CONTENTS

1
Introducing Mallorca and Menorca

Visited by wave after wave of would-be conquerers throughout the centuries, the Balearic islands today bask peacefully in the Mediterranean sun, the only invasion coming from the sun-loving tourists. Mallorca and Menorca, the two largest islands, are quite different in character. Mallorca is like an unrolled parchment, with the jagged limestone peaks of the Tramuntana mountains to the west and undulating hills to the east framing a flat central plain. Menorca is softer and greener, with near-deserted white beaches and turquoise water, its grassy meadows inland dotted with spectacular stone structures dating back to the Bronze Age.

Mallorca is the livelier of the two, most of the holiday resorts radiating east and west around the bay named after the elegant capital, **Palma**. A glamorous yachting set rubs shoulders with royalty in the seafood restaurants around the marina, while further west the towns of **Magaluf** and **Palma Nova** are non-stop action, crowds flocking to the wide, sandy beaches and sparkling nightlife. Other visitors scatter to the huge bay of Alcúdia in the north, or to luxury country estates.

Largely protected from development, **Menorca** is a haven for nature-lovers. Peaceful holiday resorts line the mellow south coast while sleepy fishing villages are dotted along the rockier northern shore. A century of British occupation left many traces on **Maó**, its tiny capital, from bow windows to gin distilleries. **Ciutadella**, the former capital, is a charming tangle of streets, old merchants' homes and churches. Beyond the two is magnificent hiking country.

SPAIN
MENORCA
EIVISSA
MALLORCA
FORMENTERA
ALGERIA

TOP ATTRACTIONS

*** **Coves del Drac:** spectacular underground rock formations.
*** **Deià:** red-roofed artists' colony in Mallorca's pine-clad Serra de Tramuntana.
*** **Palma:** Rich Gothic and Baroque architecture overlooking the elegant bay.
*** **Torre d'en Gaumes:** one of Menorca's most mysterious prehistoric sites.
*** **Valldemossa:** where the composer Chopin passed a winter in a monk's cell.
** **Local Festivals:** revealing the islands' rich, colourful folklore.

Opposite: *The splendid beach of Santa Ponça.*

Below: *A traditional
countryside gate made
from olive wood.*

THE LAND
Mountains

Mallorca is the largest of the Balearic islands, approximately 100km (65 miles) from Sant Telm on the west to Cala Ratjada on the east coast. It offers miles of spectacular coastline and a landscape that for its size (less than 3640km²; 1405 sq miles), is both as dramatic and pastoral as you could wish for. The main mountain range, the **Serra de Tramuntana,** stretches the length of the northwestern coast, rising to the 1445m-high Puig Major (4740ft) in the centre. A gentler range, the **Serra de Llevant,** marks the southeastern coastline, its highest peak (Sant Salvador) is a mere 510m (1673ft). Between these two lies **Es Pla**, a virtually flat agricultural plain.

Most of Mallorca is easily accessible by an excellent road network which includes sweeping stretches of motorway. A few winding mountain roads may be only for the skilled or the intrepid, although the views they offer are truly spectacular.

Geographically, Menorca falls neatly into two halves: the north, a reasonably fertile area of low hills and valleys known as the **Tramunta**, and the south which consists mainly of an arid limestone plateau called the **Migjorn**. There is one mountain – perhaps more of a tall hill – **Mont Toro**, which is in the centre of Menorca. From its 358m (1175ft) peak you can see the entire island and, on a good day, Mallorca to the south. Generally the island's interior often resembles a sub-tropical version of England: a neat patchwork of fields, separated from each other by dry-stone walls and grazed on by amiable Holstein cows. There's only one major road on Menorca: the central highway that runs from Maó to Ciutadella and branches off towards the resorts.

Seas and Shores

Mallorca has a varied and dramatic coastline. Two huge bays have been gnawed out of the island by wind and wave: the **Badia d'Alcúdia** in the north and the **Badia de Palma** in the southwest. Time and the weather have carved hundreds of extraordinary valleys out of the mainly limestone rock: don't miss the immense caves at **Drac**, **Artà** and **Hams**.

On the west and northwest of the island, the great cliffs of the Tramuntana mountains plunge down to the sea. Hundreds of hidden coves pepper the calmer eastern shore. In the north and south are gentle sandy beaches that attract the most tourists; off the southern shore lies the mini-archipelago of **Cabrera**, once a prison and now a nature park.

Menorca lies 225km (140 miles) southeast of Barcelona and 34km (21 miles) northeast of Mallorca. Measuring 48km (29 miles) long from east to west, its width varies from 10–19km (6–12 miles) wide, north to south. This gives Menorca a coastline of 200km (124 miles), with more accessible beaches and coves than all the other Balearic islands put together. *Calas*, or coves, are the most significant coastal feature, terminating in sandy beaches. These lie at the end of ravines (*barrancos*).

Above: *The Balearics are ringed by breathtakingly dramatic coastal scenery.*

AGROTURISMO

'Agrotourism' is a buzzword in many European countries and, broadly speaking, translates as 'rural tourism' – getting visitors to experience life in the country away from the tourist ghettos. Agrotourism is sometimes supported by government grants. The Balearic islands have an active agrotourism association which produces a guide to *fincas* (farms of country estates) which accept guests. Emphasis is on local, often organically produced food and many of the *fincas* are in beautiful, remote areas. One in Mallorca, **Son Bascos**, is a working quail farm where guests can join a hunting expedition if they wish.

WETLAND BIRDS

Herons, egrets, bitterns, stints, curlews, terns and warblers – and that's only a fraction of them! Among the best sites for birdwatching are the reserve at **S'Albufera** and the **Salines de Llevant** on Menorca. Sadly, the marshes and wetlands are often most under threat from developers, who argue that since they are not arable land, some other use should be made of them. The Toucan marsh at Alcúdia has already been destroyed; the fight continues over Sa Dragonera.

Climate

Mallorca offers a near-classic Mediterranean climate. Winters are mild, summers hot and dry. Yet the peaks of the Serra de Tramuntana may sometimes be snow-clad in winter, even as warm sunshine floods the lower valleys. The mountains in general protect the island from the seasonal cool, northern winds, so there is considerably more rainfall on both the western and eastern slopes. Mallorca's coastline often appears to escape the worst of the summer heat by virtue of cooling sea breezes. The centre of the island can be extremely hot from the end of June to September.

Lacking a similar mountain range, Menorca's climate is far more typical of the region; the far smaller interior, too, can become extremely hot at the height of summer. Without a mountain range there is no appreciable rain shadow, so the land is far drier – and often, in winter, far cooler than Mallorca.

Plantlife

One of the lasting memories for anyone visiting Mallorca in spring is the sea of pink and white almond blossom stretching across the Central Plain. Shady orange and lemon groves cling to terraced plots in the steep foothills of the Serra de Tramuntana and gnarled olive trees yield plump fruit, a feature of the robust Mallorquin cuisine. High in the mountains, the clear air is scented with pines and on the hot plain, carob trees are distinguishable by their waxy, bottle-green leaves.

COMPARATIVE CLIMATE CHART	PALMA				MAO				BARCELONA			
	WIN JAN	SPR APR	SUM JULY	AUT OCT	WIN JAN	SPR APR	SUM JULY	AUT OCT	WIN JAN	SPR APR	SUM JULY	AUT OCT
MAX TEMP. °C	15	22	28	19	13	21	27	19	14	21	27	17
MIN TEMP. °C	7	13	19	11	8	14	20	11	7	14	20	11
MAX TEMP. °F	60	72	83	66	58	71	81	65	57	71	80	62
MIN TEMP. °F	44	56	67	51	46	57	68	52	46	58	68	52
HOURS OF SUN	6	9	9	5	5	8	9	4	5	8	9	4
RAINFALL in	1.4	1.0	1.1	2.1	2.1	1.3	1.3	3.7	1.6	1.7	2.1	2.4
RAINFALL mm	37	23	28	52	52	32	32	94	41	45	52	62

Mallorca and Menorca are home to an astonishing variety of flowers, among them lavender, juniper, myrtle, camomile, wild marigolds, gladioli, assorted orchids and scarlet poppies that enrich the landscape with wonderful blazes of colour. Wild rosemary, thyme, fennel and garlic scent the hedgerows in summer and in the villages, geraniums bloom scarlet in window boxes. The wetlands of S'Albufera in Mallorca's northeast and the scrub-covered dunes of the south form miniature eco-systems of their own. Menorca, meanwhile, has its own marsh area, also called S'Albufera, populated by tamarisk trees and a wide variety of birdlife.

A Dog's Life

Watch out for the local breed of dog, called *ca de bestiar*, now almost extinct, but rather similar to a black Labrador. It's reputed to be wary of strangers but incredibly loyal to its owner and family.

Wildlife

Birds on each island are particularly spectacular and varied: Eleanora's falcons and huge black vultures, Bonelli's eagles, golden eagles and ospreys wheel high above Mallorca's Serra de Tramuntana while bee-catchers, hoopoes and a bewildering variety of sea and song birds all have their own special habitats. The wetlands attract flamingo, curlew, sandpiper, mallard, pipit, heron and moorhen, while Menorca is the only breeding place in the Balearics of the Egyptian vulture. Sadly, the islanders have a taste for songbirds and thrush and blackbird are illegally hunted. Woodcock, turtle dove and quail are also destined for the cooking pot in season.

Animal life includes rabbits, Spanish hares and weasels, as well as hedgehogs and bats. All four species of snake found here are harmless and there are several interesting lizards, including the rare star lizard, only found on Menorca. Wild tortoises and turtles still breed on Menorca, although their numbers are diminishing.

Opposite: *A field of corn poppies adds a brilliant splash of colour to Mallorca's landscape.*
Below: *An osprey glides above Mallorca's coast.*

HISTORY IN BRIEF

Prehistory c. 4000BC–1200BC

The earliest traces of human habitation in the Balearics were found in a cave near Sóller in Mallorca, dating back to about 4000BC. These first inhabitants probably came from the Iberian peninsula and were hunter-gatherers who lived in caves. They started to build simple stone houses from about 3000BC onwards and around the same time began keeping domestic animals and turning their attention to farming.

Talayotic Period c. 1200BC–200BC

The early stone houses became more and more elaborate and sophisticated. Around 1200BC large stone structures known as *talayots*, conical mounds of stone about 5–10m (15–30ft) high, were being built. No-one really knows what they were for, although burial chambers are often put forward as the most likely explanation. There are hundreds of talayotic sites scattered around Menorca and several on Mallorca; among the best are the **Torre d'en Gaumes** and **Capocorb Vell**.

Taulas, massive stone slabs, are only found on Menorca. Again their function is unclear, but a great deal of work went into their construction: the upright stones were set into grooved channels carved into the ground. *Taulas* are always found in settlements, never far from a *talayot*, and inside a small horseshoe-shaped enclosure. The wealth of ancient architecture on Menorca also includes *navetas* – stone burial chambers which resemble upturned boats.

Trade Wars and the Carthaginians

For a thousand years the Mediterranean witnessed a series of trade wars between the Minoan-Cretan, Greek, Phoenician (from what is now the Lebanon), Carthaginian (from North Africa) and Roman empires. Initially the Balearics were only marginally involved,

HISTORICAL CALENDAR

4000BC–1200BC First settlers in the Balearics (cave-dwellers).
1200BC First *talayots* built.
123BC Roman general Quintus Caecilius Metullus conquers the Balearics and names them; founds capital Palma, on Mallorca.
848 Balearics become part of Caliphate of Córdoba, ruled by the Moors.
1229 Jaume I of Aragón lands at Santa Ponça and takes back the island from the Moors as part of the *Reconquista*. Moors and islanders coexist peacefully.

1272 Mallorca established as independent kingdom.
1287 Menorca falls to Alfons III of Aragón, who defeats and expels the Moors.
1349 Jaume III killed at Llucmajor; Mallorca becomes part of Aragón.
1500–1700 Balearics neglected as Spain discovers New World.
1708 British conquer Menorca.
1808–1815 Mallorca used as a prisoner-of-war camp during Napoleonic Wars.
19th century Influx of aristocracy and intellectuals.

1930 Hotel Formentor opens on Mallorca's northernmost tip.
1936–39 Spanish Civil War: Mallorca supports Nationalists, Menorca Republicans.
1960s Mallorca developed for big tourism boom.
1983 Palma becomes the capital of the new Spanish autonomous region of the Balearic Islands.
1990s Big rebuilding program to upgrade Palma Nova and Magaluf.
1999 Spain joins European Monetary union.

as sailors preferred to hug the main coastline. But as shipbuilding and navigation techniques improved, the natural harbours offered by the islands – especially Maó in Menorca – became ever more valuable.

Greeks and Phoenicians set up trading posts and small colonies on the islands. The Balearics then became part of the **Carthaginian** trading empire and most of the major ports were founded (Maó takes its name from Hannibal's brother, Mago, who landed here in 206BC). Meanwhile the islanders had developed a fearsome weapon of war – the **slingshot**, used to project stones and flaming missiles against the enemy. Balearic sharp-shooters were famous for carrying one sling in the hand, with a second wrapped around the waist and a third around their heads. The word 'Balearis' is thought to come from the Greek *ballein* (slingshot), and thousands of local slingers were recruited into the Carthaginian army. However, effective as these soldiers were, they were no match for the highly-trained Roman army. In 146BC Carthage was defeated by Rome, though it took another 20 years for the Romans to press home their advantage in the Balearics.

Opposite: *Menorca is littered with prehistoric remains such as these found at Trepucó.*
Below: *Ancient troglodyte dwellings at Cala Morell, Menorca, some of the most important late Bronze Age caves in Europe.*

Roman Occupation 123BC–c. AD425

A Roman legion led by general **Quintus Caecilius
Metullus** invaded and conquered Mallorca in 123BC.
Once in posession, the Romans renamed the islands
Balearis Major and **Balearis Minor**, which have been
transformed over the years into Majorca and Menorca. The
islanders continued to live in villages around the *talayots*
and there's scant evidence that the Romans indulged in
the rash of building and public works that usually
characterised their occupation. The small amphitheatre at
Alcúdia is one of the few extant Roman buildings in the
Balearics. They did, however, found the city of Palma.

Following the disintegration of the Roman Empire in
the 5th century the Balearics came under the control of
different 'barbarian' tribes such as the Goths and the
Vandals, until the latter were expelled from the islands
by an expedition mounted by the Byzantine Empire in
AD534. Then began three hundred years of relative
peace and prosperity. While much of mainland Spain
suffered under the increasingly erratic rule of the
Visigoths, the Balearics were left to develop a quieter
and more civilized existence.

Opposite: *Ramón Llull,
13th-century Mallorcan
scholar and missionary.*
Below: *The tiny amphitheatre near Alcúdia
provides one of the
few remaining traces
of Roman occupation.*

The Balearics under the Moors 848–1229

For thousands of years North Africa had been ruled
by foreigners – Phoenicians, Romans, Vandals and
Byzantines – until taken over by Islamic Arabs in the 7th
century. Muslim converts
in North Africa became
known as the **Moors**. In 711
a Moorish army landed at
Gibraltar; within seven
years almost all of main-
land Spain was under
Moorish control, which
became known as the
Caliphate of Córdoba.
At first the caliphs were
content to accept tribute
from the Balearics but in

848 they sent in their navy to quell island rebellions and then moved in. Under the Moors, the Balearics had a degree of local self-government, but the occupation also established the legal precedent that the Balearics belonged to Spain itself – until then, they had been accepted as a different country.

Palaces, mosques and gardens were built; arts and education flourished. Agriculture also benefitted: almond trees, figs, carobs, apricots and peaches were planted, while technological innnovations to help cultivation, such as wind-mills and waterwheels, were introduced. The **Banys Arabs**, or Arab Baths, in Palma are a small reminder of what life was probably like: having gained a country the Moors were determined to turn it into a paradise. But eventually the Moors lost their fighting edge and the Middle East was no longer willing or able to send troops.

The Reconquista

Determined to bring control of Spain back into Christian hands, **Jaume I** of Aragón landed at Santa Ponça on 10 September 1229 with 16,000 men, supported by 500 ships. Outnumbered but battle-hardened, Jaume's troops took Palma on 31 December. However, he came to an arrange-ment with the Moors of Menorca, accepting an annual tribute in return for leaving them in peace. The Moors stayed in Menorca until 1287, when Alfons III of Aragón invaded and defeated them.

Mallorca continued to prosper under Jaume I's enlight-ened rule. These years heralded a golden age, when the realization of independence resulted in an outpouring of nationalist pride and culture. Jaume I divided his lands between his sons in 1272, creating a separate kingdom of Mallorca. The subsequent dynastic squabble lasted until 1349, when Jaume III was killed in battle at Llucmajor and the Balearics passed back into the control of Aragón. The Balearics now came under **Aragón**'s total dominance and acquired the Catalan language, from which Mallorquí and Menorquí are derived.

RAMON LLULL

Self-styled missionary and 13th-century scholar Ramón Llull is Mallorca's most famous son, as much for his prolific writing as for his religious zeal. Originally a wealthy family man who scandalized society by falling in love with a married woman, Llull converted to Christianity aged 40. He studied Arabic and, aged 60, travelled throughout the Middle East and Africa converting Muslims to the Christian faith. Whether he was successful is not known but his 6000 proverbs survive to this day, covering every-thing from astronomy to horsemanship and providing a fascinating insight into Mallorcan social history in the Middle Ages.

Above: *'El Conqueridor' Jaume I of Aragón, who recaptured Mallorca from the Moors.*

TERRIBLE TURKS

Like most Mediterranean islands in the 16th century, Menorca had a rough time at the hands of Turkish pirates. Turkish admiral and pirate Kheir-ed-Din – otherwise known as **Barbarossa** (redbeard) – sailed into Maó harbour in September 1535 on a revenge raid. Thanks to a treacherous Menorcan official the town gates were opened to him. Barbarossa sacked Maó and made off with 800 prisoners, destined to become slaves.

Ciutadella fared even worse. In 1558 the Turkish **Admiral Piali** razed the city to the ground and carried off all its 3500 inhabitants – including the governor.

Meanwhile, mainland Spain was continuing the *Reconquista* designed to unite the country. **Ferdinand of Aragón** married **Isabel of Castile** in 1469; the last Moorish outpost of Granada fell to their armies in 1492 and the Balearics were now part of the new Spain.

Columbus discovered the Americas in 1492 and Spain immediately turned her attentions westwards, to the **New World** and beyond. The Balearics were largely forgotten, except as a source of men for the armies that were slowly establishing Spain's new frontiers. Soon both Turkish raiders and the Mediterranean's **pirates** were more or less attacking at will – Barbarossa sacked Maó on Menorca in 1535 and Ciutadella three years later. Spain did not attempt to put an end to the pirates until the end of the 16th century, causing deep resentment among the islanders.

French and British Ties

The Spanish Empire collapsed in 1700, when the imbecilic Carlos II died without leaving an heir. This was followed by the **War of the Spanish Succession**, when the major European powers fought for control over Spain. In 1708 **Britain** seized Menorca and moored her navy in the magnificent harbour at Maó. The British stayed in Menorca for 100 years, apart from brief periods when control of the island passsed to the French and then the Spanish. Menorca was finally ceded to Spain under the **Treaty of Amiens** in 1802, but the years of occupation established an infrastructure and economic prosperity still in evidence today.

Spanish history in the 19th century is characterized by a series of uprisings, the loss of her overseas empire, political crisis and virtual anarchy. During the **Napoleonic Wars** she became a vassal state of France and was then dependent on England to regain her independence. Spain became a provincial backwater, and perhaps Mallorca would have slept its way into the future if it hadn't been discovered by the European intelligentsia and aristocracy.

Early Tourists

Frédérick Chopin and his mistress, the writer George Sand, arrived in Mallorca in 1838. Chopin appears to have fallen in love with the island from the first; George Sand cordially loathed it and its people. However, they did bring the island to the attention of the outside world, notably Archduke Louis Salvador of Austria, who became the first of many distinguished expatriates.

Tourism is often seen as being a recent Mallorcan phenomenon. In fact, Palma's **Grand Hotel** was built in 1903 and in 1905, the first Tourist Bureau was established, with brochures being sent to Thomas Cook. In 1930, the world-famous **Hotel Formentor** was built on the northernmost tip of the island by an Argentinian entrepreneur, soon attracting people like King Edward VII and the Aga Khan. But this triumph was followed by disaster: the Spanish Civil War.

The Balearics and the Franco Era

Despite their common, Catalan heritage, Mallorca supported the Nationalist (General Francisco Franco's) side, whereas its sister island, Menorca, was fervently Republican. Many Mallorcans had done extremely well in banking, industry, commerce and public life on the mainland – Don Valeriano Weyler was one of Spain's most distinguished statesmen; Don Antonio Maura became Prime Minister no less than five times – so perhaps it was natural for Mallorca's elite to side with Madrid rather than Barcelona. But following a brief declaration of support, Franco sent troops to seize Mallorca and then used the island as a base from which to attack the Republicans. Italian aircraft were sent from Palma to bomb Barcelona airport; aid from Italy and Germany led to Franco's eventual victory and in 1939 he proclaimed himself head of state.

> **SOLDIERS ON CABRERA**
>
> Some 9000 French soldiers were imprisoned on Cabrera after being defeated by the Spanish army at the Battle of Bailén in 1808. Conditions were appalling and the prisoners lived rough on the island until barracks were built, eating rats and dry bread and resorting, with disastrous results, to drinking seawater when the rations ran out. When the soldiers were taken to France five years later, over 5000 had died. The crumbling *castillo* is all that remains.
>
> Today the island is a national park, protected as one of the last wilderness areas of the Mediterranean. Having been declared a military zone in 1916, Cabrera mercifully missed the tourism boom and several important species of reptile and marine life have thrived here.

Below: *Sa Cartuja, Valldemossa, winter refuge of Frédérick Chopin and George Sand.*

Thousands of Republicans were imprisoned and executed. The islands' indigenous culture was suppressed and censorship rigorously enforced. Spain remained neutral in World War II and the country was economically and politically isolated. However, a series of American loans in the 1950s rejuvenated the Spanish economy and money was then poured into tourism.

The Islands Today

When Spain as a whole began to realise the benefits of tourism in the mid-1950s, Mallorca was singled out for special development by Franco. Property developers appeared in droves, closely followed by tour operators. What the early conquerors failed to do threatened to become reality: the destruction of the Mallorcan way of life and sense of values. Despite this, the Balearics are increasingly moving upmarket and into 'green' tourism; the tourism mistakes of the past have been recognised and largely rectified, and today there is a powerful environmental lobby. Social problems, however, remain an issue, particularly on Mallorca, where a huge influx of German and British home-owners is driving property prices out of reach of the locals.

Right: *The luxurious Hotel Formentor, holiday haven for the international jet set.*
Opposite: *Consolat del Mar, Palma, once the maritime law court and now seat of the Balearic Islands' government.*

GOVERNMENT AND ECONOMY

The Balearic Islands – Mallorca, Menorca, Eivissa (Ibiza) and Formentera – are part of Spain and have comprised one **autonomous community** since 1983. Today Spain consists of 17 autonomous communities, which are quasi-federal bodies with wide ranging powers of home rule. Spain has a **democracratic parliamentary system** and a constitutional monarchy, ruled by King Juan Carlos, who is also Commander-in-Chief of the armed forces.

The regional capital of the Balearics is Palma, where the Govern Balear meets. Mallorca has the highest number of seats, with 33, Menorca has 12, Eivissa 11 and Formentera has three. Thus Mallorca is by far the senior partner but the other islands have kept their own separate and strong identities. The dominant political parties are the socialist PSOE (Partido Socialista Obrero Espanyol) and the liberal alliance PP-UM (Partido Popular-Union Mallorquína), who between them sweep up three-quarters of the votes.

The combined population of the Balearics is 745,000, of whom 325,000 live in Palma de Mallorca. Mallorca boasts the highest standard of living in Spain outside Madrid or Barcelona: car ownership is regarded as the norm by most families – an average of one car for every three local inhabitants; home ownership is increasing and a high proportion of spending goes on consumer durables. Education is compulsory from 6–16, and young Spanish males have to do national service. Tourism is taught at Mallorca's university and a private tourist school at Palma attracts hundreds of students from around the world.

Agriculture

For the most part, day-to-day agricultural management is in the hands of the older generation, while their children work in one or other of the resorts. This explains the often-deserted atmosphere of small towns and villages inland,

---

ETIQUETTE

All over Mallorca, locals are used to tourists but in some of the tiny villages on the plain, visitors are less common. Everywhere, but especially in these villages, it is polite to observe basic etiquette and a few words of Spanish or Mallorqui go a long way. *Buenos días* (good morning) or *buenas tardes* (good afternoon) should always begin a conversation, or in Mallorqui, *bon dia* and *bones tardes*. *Hola* (hello) is less formal. To thank someone for directions, say *gracias* (or *gràcies*). Don't walk around a village in swimwear; dress with respect in churches; and do not photograph people without politely asking first.

Right: *A luxury liner and fishing nets drying in the sun: symbols of tourism and traditional economic mainstays.*

with the young in school and the next generation at work some kilometres away. Yet agriculture still plays a vital role in Mallorca's economy: almonds are a valuable export, as are salad crops and root vegetables. Citrus fruits, pears, peaches, apples and figs are mainly for local and tourist consumption, while livestock is dominated by pig farming, although goats and cattle are reared by local cooperatives.

Vineyards are found around Binissalem and Felanitx and the quality of the local wine has improved beyond all recognition. Olives are widely grown, especially near the mountains, not for producing oil but for eating.

Industry

Approximately two-thirds of the population work in tourist-related service industries. Local industry centres on the tourist trade: apart from the obvious service industries, this also encompasses construction and manufacture (shoes, clothes and crafts, for example). Artisans are encouraged to make the souvenirs that tourists will want to take home, like the artificial pearls produced at Manacor or hand-blown glass. Shoe-making remains one of Menorca's major industries.

THE PEOPLE

Temperaments vary surprisingly between one Balearic island and the next and a Mallorcan will have a sense of humour quite different from his neighbour in Menorca. Both, however, are renowned for their sense of hospitality and their unflappable nature, a useful asset in the face of the annual tourist invasion. Like other Spaniards, the people of the Balearics place great importance on the family and will always include children in everything they do, which helps to explain the islands' popularity with families.

Balearic islanders seem less flamboyant than mainland Spaniards and perhaps the overwhelming impression gained is one of extreme calm. Impatient visitors sometimes assume that Balearic society is a closed shop to outsiders and that islanders distrust the bigger world. But the visitor who shows patience and understanding, and the same quiet courtesy that personifies much of Balearic life, will in turn realise how much the islanders welcome and treasure their guests. There is also a great number of expatriates, many of whom are fully integrated into the islands' communities.

CATALAN SPEAKERS

There are approximately six million people who claim Catalan as their mother tongue. They are to be found in the Balearics, Catalonia, Andorra, along the Spanish coast from Barcelona to Valencia and in the French province of Pyrenées-Orientales. French and Italian speakers will recognise many words, as will those who learned Latin at school, for Catalan is one of the purest Romance languages left in the world today. There is a close relationship between Catalan and medieval French, which gives rise to the thesis of an ancient, northwestern Mediterranean culture.

Below: *Locals relax in time-honoured fashion in the afternoon shade.*

Language

The majority of inhabitants speak Castilian Spanish, conversing with one another in their own Mallorquí and Menorquí dialects and addressing visitors in good English, German or French. Many visitors think that Mallorquí and Menorquí are separate languages in their own right, but they are dialects of Catalan and are undergoing an enthusiastic revival, following years of suppression during the Franco regime. Place and street names are rapidly being renamed in the Mallorquí or Menorquí original. Thus Andraix is now Andratx; Bañalbufar is Banyalbulfar; San Juan is Sant Joan; *cuevas* (caves) are *coves; puerto* (port) becomes *port.* The written

WITCHCRAFT

There have long been rumours about an 'earlier' pagan religion, one that pre-dated Christianity, that has somehow managed to survive. A good deal of folk-lore does stretch back for thousands of years – but anyone expecting to find a flourishing coven on the island will be disappointed.

difference is rarely enough to confuse the visitor. However, pronunciation is another matter: *x* sounds like *sh*, *-ig* at the end of a word is usually *-tch*, as in *puig* (mountain), which is pronounced *pootch*.

Throughout this book, where possible, Catalan spellings have been used for place names. The vocabulary given is generally in Castilian, except in cases of food and drink when it is a local speciality.

Religion

Catholicism is the main religion throughout the Balearics. Since the death of Franco the church has not so much declined as changed in the way it influences life and events. Today it is far less traditional than before, although many islanders appreciate its innate conservatism. Well over 50,000 islanders make an annual pilgrimage to Lluc and thousands of people will visit an obscure sanctuary on one of the many saints' days.

Mallorca is dotted with out-of-the-way sanctuaries, shrines and chapels, many of them built on the site of former Moorish mosques or much earlier, pagan, temples. However, a growing expatriate population means that

Below: *Doorway of the massive La Seu Cathedral, Palma, a testament to the enduring influence of the Catholic Church.*

other religions and their places of worship, ranging from Anglicanism to Judaism are also present. Tourist offices will have a list of what other religious services are available and some of the larger Catholic churches hold services in English.

Both Mallorcans and Menorcans expect visitors to treat their churches with respect. Sensible, modest dress is always advisable and it's only courteous to avoid sightseeing a specific church when a service is being held.

Festivals

If at first sight the Balearics, especially Mallorca, seem both polyglot and cosmopolitan, the real culture of the islands is unique and great fun. One of the more dismal aspects of Franco's dictatorship was the banning of many local fiestas. These are now celebrated with gusto and if your visit coincides with one, you're in for an unforgettable treat.

Left: Dazzling displays of equestrian skill make Menorcan fiestas even more memorable.

CALENDAR OF EVENTS

5 January Arrival of the Three Kings giving out toys and sweets; lots of fireworks and music.

16–17 January Sant Antoni: bonfires, dancing, processions, blessing of animals and folk dancing.

February Carnival: fancy dress processions.

March/April Holy Week torchlight processions in traditional costume.

23–24 June Sant Joan: week of lively fiestas, particularly in Ciutadella (superb horseriding displays).

29 June Sant Pere (patron saint of fishermen): food, dancing, and boat processions in various seaside villages.

16 July Virgin del Carmen: popular seaside festival.

24–26 July Sant Jaume: best fiestas are at Alcúdia, Villa Carlos and Sóller with devil dancing, bullfights and fireworks.

August International Music Festivals at Palma, Pollença and Deià.

end September Binissalem wine festival; a week-long fiesta after the harvest.

31 October Eve of All Saint's Day: witches, warlocks and devils dance. Shops sell imitation rosaries made of sweets.

It seems that nearly every day is a saint's day, with a fiesta going on somewhere in the islands. In practice, islanders limit themselves to around 24 fiestas throughout the year, on top of the 17 Spanish public holidays. Fiestas are generally times of processions, fireworks, food, drink, music and dance, with gaily costumed islanders having a whale of a time – don't miss the opportunity to join in. Dates for most festivals are fluid; if the actual date falls on a Tuesday or Thursday, islanders tend to bridge the fiesta with a weekend of merrymaking. The busiest time of year for fiestas is between June and September.

Although historic events and country traditions are the highlight of many fiestas, the inspiration behind most festivals is religous. The **Semana Santa** (Holy Week) processions are spectacular, albeit on the solemn side. Penitents wear tall, pointed hoods redolent of the Inquisition, while women in mantillas carry holy statues and paintings down narrow streets, all to the sound of muffled drums.

CYCLING

Tourists from all over Europe take to the roads on two wheels in spring, when the fields and hedgerows are bright with blossom and wildflowers. Cycling is a big sport in Mallorca and bicycles can be hired from most resorts – all you need is a hat, some sunblock and a water bottle. Mountain bikes are necessary to tackle the Tramuntana mountain range, but inland the country roads criss-crossing the Central Plain are equally pleasurable and very quiet. The tourist office produces a useful guide of 10 cycle tours which includes some interesting off-road diversions for you to follow.

Music and Dance

Traditional music and dance play a vital role in Mallorcan and Menorcan life. Hotels provide musical entertainment for their guests not so much because it's the fashion, but because it would be almost unthinkable not to do so.

Balearic folk dances offer an extraordinary variation of steps and movement, with *boleros*, *fandangos* and *sotas* the most popular and energetic. Dances like *es cossiers* and *es cavallets* feature horned demons; other dances represent the olive or fig harvests. The *ball d'es cossil* is a unique Menorcan dance similar to Scottish dancing. If you don't manage to see some folk dancers at a fiesta, there are regular exhibitions at **Valldemossa** and **Sa Granja**.

Many of the songs, like much Spanish folk music, owe an obvious debt to the Moorish influence. Others are attributable to the Provençal and Catalan troubadours of the Middle Ages. Balearic music initially seems to have a great deal in common with mainland Spain but some differences include the use of the *espasi*, a local drum, the *xeremia*, which can loosely be called a flute, and a type of bagpipe called *es chirimillero*, usually played on its own.

Sports

Sling-shot contests are among the most fascinating of all traditional pastimes. Competitions are held regularly in Palma de Mallorca; Spanish or Catalan-speaking visitors may even be able to learn something of the art for themselves. Some idea of how seriously the island takes this is shown by the statue to Mallorca's *honderos* (slingers) in the S'Hort del Rei (King's Gardens).

Football is one pastime that unites all Mallorcans, be it playing or watching. Every village has its own team; better club matches are held at the Estadio Balear i Luis Sitjar in Palma.

There are all kinds of **watersports** on offer in the Balearics, from swimming, to waterskiing, to scuba diving and sailing. Fishing tackle is widely available and inexpensive. Alternatively, get away from it all and hire a boat to explore idyllic, sandy coves.

Bullfighting

Summer is the season for bullfights, which take place in Palma and other Mallorcan towns but not on Menorca. Regarded by the Spanish as an art form rather than a sport, if you wish to go to a *corrida* choose your seat carefully: *sol* means you'll be in the blazing sun, *ombre* in the shade and *sol y ombre* a mixture of both. Naturally, the shady seats are the most expensive.

Horses

You can hire horses at many resorts for a trot on the beach or a trek into the hinterland. For spectators, trotting races – where the jockey sits behind the horse in a small cart – are very popular and are held year-round at Son Pardo near Palma, and Maó and Ciutadella. If you're in Menorca, a typical spectacle is a kind of dressage, often demonstrated at island fiestas in the middle of a crowd.

Above: *Trotting races are a popular spectator sport on the islands.*
Opposite left: *Folk dancers in traditional costume enliven the island fiestas.*
Opposite right: *One traditional instrument is the* zambomba, *a type of drum.*

GOLF

For a small island, Mallorca has an impressive collection of golf courses, many of championship standard. Seven of the 10 are 18-hole and green fees are very reasonable. Club hire and tuition is available at all 10. With the obvious exception of the mountains, courses are accessible from most resorts. The **Pomiente**, **Santa Ponça**, **Son Vida** and the new **Son Antem** are all within easy reach of Palma; **Capdepera Club** serves the northeast and **Val d'Or** is close to Cala d'Or in the east.

Architecture

Popular island architecture is characterized by low-rise, whitewashed limestone houses, many of them following the Moorish design of rooms opening onto a central patio with a fountain. Various luminaries, however, have left their mark on some of the island's more unusual buildings. Antoni Gaudí, the famous and controversial Catalunyan architect, came to Mallorca in 1902 to help restore Palma's cathedral and the results of his work can be seen today over the high altar. Local architects followed Gaudí's Modernista style and the brilliant mosaic pattern on Casa Forteza Rey in Palma, designed by silversmith Lluis Forteza Rey, is reminiscent of some of the bizarre colours and twists of buildings in Barcelona.

Most of Mallorca's architectural treasures are in **Palma**, including **La Seu Cathedral**, the **Almudaina Palace** and the magnificent, Gothic **Sa Llotja**, built by Mallorquín Guillem Sagrera in the 15th century and used today as an exhibition centre. There are, however, some beautiful old country mansions to explore, including the crumbling **Alfabia** near Sóller in the west, an old Moorish palace with charming gardens.

In Menorca, look out for British influences in some of the older buildings; in Maó, there are several fine examples of sash windows, Georgian fanlights and cast iron balustrades. In Villa Carlos (also known as Es Castell, or Georgetown), outside Maó, the elegant façades of the British barracks and the Georgian town hall would be equally appropriate in London.

Art in Mallorca

Mallorca has long been attracting artists from abroad, such as Joan Miró (1893–1983) and has developed more than a few of its own. The present-day rising star Miquel Barcó, darling of the New York art world, was born in Felanitx.

Mountain villages like Deià and Sant Vicenç are still artistic enclaves, although perhaps these days they are less bohemian and more expensive than before. Pollença holds an annual painting competition and there are over 20 art galleries in Palma alone that carry local artists' work. If you want to check out what's happening on the art scene, the Independent Association of Balearic Art Galleries produces a bi-monthly gallery and exhibition list.

Mallorcans themselves are well educated in the fine arts and support them with a knowledgeable enthusiasm. The island abounds with *domingueros*, effectively Sunday painters of the sea and landscape. However it is the *jovenes*, young painters, whose work and exploits have captured the hearts and imaginations of much of the population. Local newspapers carry regular articles on their progress; at times they seem to be treated like rock stars.

MODERNISTA ARCHITECTURE

The highlight of Spanish architecture over the past few hundred years has been Modernista, an essentially Catalunyan version of Art Nouveau. Modernista's greatest exponent was architect **Antoni Gaudí**, and you can see examples of his work in La Seu Cathedral, Palma and Lluc monastery. One of Gaudi's pupils was the Mallorcan **Joan Rubió** – don't miss his work in Sóller (*see* p. 57).

Opposite: *Rounded arches and ornate balconies are typically Moorish, adapted for Balearic architecture.* **Below:** *The artist's studio at the Fundació Pilar i Joan Miró near Palma.*

Above left: *Sturdy terracotta pots make charming souvenirs.*
Above right: *Mallorca's unique fragile clay figures known as* siurells.

NIGHTLIFE

The club scene in Mallorca is fast and furious. Get up early at the weekend and people will still be strolling home from the nightclubs. Even if you're not a clubber, some places are worth a visit for the sheer spectacle. **BCM** in Magaluf claims to be Europe's largest disco and has dance floors on several levels playing anything from acid house to eighties hits, with lavish laser shows. **Tito's,** on the Passeig Maritimo is a glitzy hall of mirrors reached by a glass elevator with stunning views of the harbour lights. Alternatively, wander around the district of **La Lonja**, which is always buzzing with life until the early hours.

Crafts

With the change of emphasis from mass-market to up-market tourism, there's an increasing demand for well made, local goods. Old crafts and traditions are being revised, while those that survived the initial tourist onslaught have gone from strength to strength. Traditional craft bargains include Manacor artificial pearls (*see* p. 100) and baskets made from palm leaves; others include the following:

Leather

Mallorca and Menorca are famous for their leather and suede – bags, shoes and clothes are particularly good buys. You can visit factories in Inca on Mallorca and in Ciutadella and Alaior on Menorca. While goods aren't as cheap as the used to be, they're still a fraction of the price you'd pay back home.

Pottery

Throughout Mallorca you'll find handmade, fragile clay figures known as *siurells*. These are ancient gifts of friendship – sometimes fertility charms – that have been made for thousands of years. They have a whistle built into the base and are painted white with splashes of a particularly vivid green or red.

Although not quite so old, **majolica wall tiles** have been delighting visitors for hundreds of years. Typically designed in bold blue and white, they feature scenes from island life, or from Cervantes' *Don Quixote*. At Felanitx, in the east of the island, semi-glazed brown pots, and other tableware are produced in designs that range from the ornate to the simple.

Carving

Olive wood is carved into a wonderful variety of household utensils. These might look purely decorative, courtesy of the golden colour and swirling grain of the wood, but they are eminently practical: olive wood is strong and hard-wearing.

Weaving

Look for *roba de llengües* (cloth of tongues), a hard-wearing cotton cloth decorated with a zig-zag pattern in bold, primary reds, blues or greens. A wonderfully versatile material, this cloth can be used for everything from bedspreads to wall hangings.

Glassblowing

Mallorcan glass used to rival Venetian in terms of quality, but it came dangerously close to dying out. It is now enjoying a welcome renaissance and it is well worth a special visit to the various workshops and factories, such as Casa Gordiola at Algaida (*see* p. 99).

LOCAL LIQUORS

Walk into most Spanish bars and you will be greeted by a diverse and welcoming collection of different bottles. Mallorca is no different, the island's own contribution being *hierbas*, liqueurs based on herbs and aniseed, while Menorca supplies a distinctive and excellent gin – the **Xoriguer** brands are probably the best. *Hierbas* can be sweet or dry and free tastings can be arranged, particularly with the **Tunel** range. These take place at various *bodegas*, or distillery/vineyards, and even souvenir shops. A liqueur called *palo*, made from fermented carob beans, is widely drunk with black coffee, as is Spanish brandy.

Left: *The ancient art of glassblowing still thrives on Mallorca.*
Below: *Lovely Mallorcan hand-blown glass comes in a wide variety of shapes and colours.*

Below: *An enticing
variety of local produce
for sale.*

Food and Drink

Away from the fast food and bland international
buffets of the big tourist resorts, gourmet dishes from
the regions of Spain are widely available, particularly
in Palma. Genuine Mallorcan cuisine is not especially
refined, based largely on the peasant fare on which
the islanders survived in their turbulent past. The
popularity of pork, rabbit and *caracoles*, or snails, gives
a clue to the kind of food that has been available here
throughout the ages.

Portions tend to be large and robust, based around big,
meaty stews, *pa amb oli* (bread spread with olive oil and
tomatoes) and pork products preserved with spices. More
subtle dishes such as the ubiquitous *paella* and *gazpacho*
are imports, from Valencia and Andalucía respectively.

One of the most typical dishes is *sopas mallorquines*,
a hearty broth containing port and vegetables which is
eaten with bread. A vegetarian alternative is *tumbet*,
containing fried aubergines, peppers
and potatoes. The squeamish should
watch out for *frito mallorquín*, which may
sound like a good fry-up but features
liver, lungs and blood. *Asados de lechona*,
roast suckling pig, is a popular main
course, as is *lomo con col*, or pork with
cabbage. Yet more pork is a main
ingredient of *sobrasada*, a spicy
sausage meat available everywhere.

Other specialities are restricted to
certain areas, or even towns. *Espinagada*,
eel and spinach pie, is a tradition of Sa
Pobla, while special fish pies are made
in San Joan, both on Mallorca. Fish,
incidentally, is not as widespread as
might be expected. The Mediterranean
is severely over-fished and many species
are imported from the Atlantic. *Salmonete*,
red mullet, is available locally and in
Menorca, *llagosta,* or spiny lobster, is
prolific and makes a tasty stew.

Pastries

Mallorcans have something of a sweet tooth, possibly inherited from the Moors, who used a lot of honey and almonds. Cakes and pastries are big sellers with the morning coffee. *Ensaïmada* is a sweet, lard-based pastry filled with cream or crème pâtisserie and dusted with icing sugar, while *gelato de almendra* is delicious almond ice-cream.

Menorcan cuisine is slightly richer and based more on butter and cream than olive oil. Specialities to try are the expensive *calderada de llagosta* (lobster stew) and the more modest *peix al forn amb patatas* (oven-baked fish with potatoes), or partridge with cabbage. Don't forget to try the delicious and famous cheeses, made from the milk of dairy herds raised on the island. Menorcan country women (*madones*) follow ancient recipes and traditional methods of production.

Above: *Local delicacies include the* ensaïmada, *a cream-filled pastry.*

Wine

Spanish wine is now justifiably famous the world over. Most people know of the heavily oaked Riojas from northern Spain; also well worth a try are the lighter and fresher Navarras. Local wines, mainly from Mallorca are grown on the central plain, particularly around the towns of Binissalem, Felanitx and Porreres. The island's once-famous native grape strains have never really recovered from phylloxera plague in the 1890s and Mallorcan wines are not known in Spain for their brilliance. The better labels like José Ferrer and Jaime Mesquida come straight from the *bodegas*.

Spanish *cava* (sparkling wine) can be extremely good, especially Juve y Camps, Anna Codoníu or Segura Viudas. *Cava* served by the glass in bars may be too sweet for the Northern European palate, but the *seco* or dry variety will be more than acceptable.

FABULOUS FISH

Fish is expensive but of excellent quality. The following are typical dishes of both islands:
Arroz negro • rice flavoured and coloured with squid ink
Boquerones • anchovies in batter
Calderada llagosta • lobster in tomato sauce
Gambas • large prawns
Greizonera d'anguila • eel stew
Greizonera de peix • fish stew
Lubina con sal • sea bass baked in rock salt and absolutely superb
Puntillas • baby squid
Salmontes • red mullet
Sardinas à la plancha • grilled sardines
On Menorca, lobster – expensive but delicious – may be grilled or in a *calderada* (soup).

2
Palma

Basking in the centre of the broad sweep of the Badia de Palma, Mallorca's capital is a surprisingly elegant and cosmopolitan city, its waterfront dominated by a massive Gothic cathedral and its rooftops overlooked by the stone mass of the Castell de Bellver. Palm trees flank a long, seafront boulevard and in the port, coloured fishing boats bob alongside gleaming yachts. Fishermen still dry their nets here, providing a contrast to the tourists and cars streaming off the inter-island and mainland ferries.

Palma in its present form dates back to 1230, when Jaume I recaptured Mallorca from the Moors and then tore down most of the Moorish buildings, with really only the **Banys Arabs** (Arab Baths) still surviving to this day. Among the jumble of modern buildings, however, are magnificent, 500-year-old mansions and some spectacular examples of Gothic architecture like **Sa Llotja**, now an exhibition hall, and the 17th-century Baroque **Consolat de Mar** next door.

Every possible taste is catered for along the shores of Palma's bay, from designer shops on the Avinguda del Rei Jaume III to gypsy markets. On Saturdays, shop for bargains in the **Baratillo**, the city's famous flea market where Mallorcan artificial pearls can be found at discount prices. Dining ranges from fast food to Spanish haute cuisine, while nightlife runs the gamut from the most high-tech of clubs to the romance of sipping *fino* outside a bar in the shadow of the cathedral on a hot summer's night, listening to a Spanish guitar.

MENORCA

Ciutadella

Santa
Margalida
Artà

PALMA DE
MALLORCA
Porto
Cristo

MALLORCA

CLIMATE

Expect magnificent sunshine throughout the spring, summer and autumn, with mid-summer temperatures averaging 32°C (90°F), sometimes even higher. Sheltered by the natural harbour and northern mountains, calm weather typifies this town, where even in winter temperatures stay as high as 12°C (53°F).

Opposite: *The imposing mass of La Seu Cathedral dominates Palma Bay.*

DON'T MISS

*** Baratillo: pick up a
bargain in the flea market.
*** La Seu: an absolutely
awe-inspiring cathedral.
*** Sa Llotja: make a point
of seeing Palma's graceful
Gothic stock exchange.
*** The Barri Gòtic: Palma's
ancient quarter.
** Poble Espanyol: the
best of Spanish architecture
in one village.
* Shopping: a wide selection
– from *haute couture* to flea
market bargains.

CITY SIGHTSEEING

Most of Palma's sights are located in the narrow streets
radiating out from the cathedral and can be viewed on
foot. A long stretch of palm-lined greenery follows the line
of the old city's sea walls. The western boundary of the
old town is the former Arab moat, now the promenade **Es
Born**, lined with open-air cafés and a popular meeting
place during the ritual evening stroll, or *passeig*.

Parc de la Mar ★

Near the south side of La Seu Cathedral, this tiered park
offers a relaxing introduction to Palma's waterfront.
Abstract art dotted around the park includes a tiled
mural by Joan Miró. Look out for the lake designed
to reflect the cathedral and the **Arc de la Drassana
Musulmana**, an arch that curves over a lake of black
swans – a reminder of Palma's Moorish past that was
once the gateway to the royal docks.

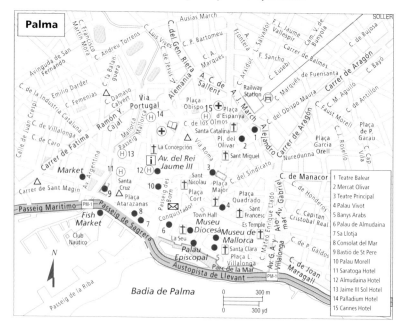

La Seu Cathedral ★★★

Described by French writer George Sand in 1838 as an 'imposing mass that rises from the sea... flanked by a great stone organ', the enormous Gothic cathedral of La Seu has been impressing people for hundreds of years. It was intended as more of a political than a religious statement, a 'here we are and here we intend to stay' shout to the Moors

Above: *Travelling in a tartana, a horse-drawn carriage, is a novel way of seeing the sights.*

or any other would-be invader. Work began in 1230 after the Christian reconquest of the city by Jaume I but was not completed until the 17th century. There was extensive restoration in the 19th century, following damage caused by an earthquake.

To many, those massive flying buttresses that so impressed George Sand are more like bars that hold captive some great, unutterably strange sea-beast. Without doubt, La Seu is best viewed from the sea by night, when floodlights turn the entire ensemble into a futuristic, almost mechanical edifice.

However, if the exterior is impressive, the interior is awe-inspiring. Enter through the 15m (50ft) tall archway and stand enthralled at the central nave soaring 44m (147ft) high, seemingly suspended in mid-air, so slender are the 14 pillars that support it. With a 13.3m (43ft) diameter, the east rose window is nearly the biggest in the world, its effect enhanced by rows of smaller stained glass windows that add to the feeling of airiness and light.

Barcelona's most famous architect, Antoni Gaudí, was asked to restore the canopy over the high altar in 1902. His *modernista* work, *Crown of Thorns*, is as controversial as his masterpiece, the church of the Sagrada Familia in Barcelona. Open 10:00–15:00 November–March; 10:00–18:00 April–October; 10:00–14:00 Saturday; closed Sundays and holidays.

ALL AT SEA

The small fishing boats are called *llauds*; the larger, catching fish more than 30km (18½ miles) offshore and often staying at sea for several days, are *barca de bou*. Both catch an astonishing range of fish, but don't expect it to be especially cheap: the Spanish are the biggest fish-eaters in Europe and the demand is great. The best fish market on Mallorca is the Tems Market, on Carrer Juan Crespi in Palma, where every stall-owner appears to be an artist, so beautifully are the days' wares put on display.

Above: *The Palau de Almudaina, used by King Juan Carlos for official business when he is in Palma.*

Museu Diocesà *
(Diocesan Museum)

This eccentric museum is located in the Palau Episcopal round the back of the cathedral. Exhibits range from a collection of auto graphs, including those of Napoleon Bonaparte and Queen Victoria, to 15th-century statues and a stuffed alligator dated 1776. Open 10:00–13:00 and 15:00–18:00 November–March; 10:00–13:00 and 15:00–20:00 April–October; weekends and holidays 10:00–13:00.

Barri Gòtic ***

Palma's Gothic Quarter is a tangle of narrow streets around the cathedral, lined by magnificent baronial houses, some over 500 years old. Some have dark walls and dense, forbidding wooden doors with brass knockers, but the occasional glimpse through an iron grille to a luxuriant central courtyard with a splashing fountain gives an idea of the sumptuous interiors of these aristocratic homes.

One old house on Carrer Sant Joan has been converted into a wonderful bar, **Abaco**, where a fashionable clientele wanders from room to room admiring antiques and flower arrangements to the sounds of opera.

Palau de Almudaina **

Opposite the cathedral stands the Palau de Almudaina, previously a Roman citadel, a Moorish palace and a king's palace. Now it houses the Museum of National Heritage and is the military headquarters of the Balearic islands. The tour includes the 13th-century throne room and the royal chapel of Santa Ana, which has an unusual, 14th-century Romanesque doorway. Open 10:00–14:00 and 16:00–18:00 October–March; 10:00–18:30 April–September; Saturdays and holidays 10:00–14:00; closed Sunday.

MOORISH PALMA

Remnants of Moorish architecture are sparse in Palma relative to cities on mainland Spain. Mallorca's spell under Islamic rule was shorter than that of the mainland at just under 400 years, from 848–1229. During this time the city was known as Medina Mayurka, its fortified walls occupying what are now Carrer Miramar and Carrer Morey and the Passeig d'es Born. Today, the only visible traces of this time are the foundations of the Almudaina Palace (*al-Medina* in Arabic means 'the city'), the old Arab Baths on Carrer Serra and an arch, the Arc de la Mar, set into the walls below the Almudaina Palace.

Sa Llotja ★★★

Sa Llotja was built as Palma's stock exchange between 1426 and 1450 by Guillem Sagrera, after whom the seafront promenade is named. An example of Gothic architecture, it is ornamented with gargoyles and topped with crenellated towers. Inside slender columns twist up to a high, vaulted roof, giving the impression of a palm grove. Christopher Columbus traded in silks here and, according to legend, also planned his voyage of discovery to the New World. Today, the building is used as an art gallery. The tourist board will provide details of exhibitions. Next to Sa Llotja, the 17th-century law court, **Consolat del Mar**, houses the autonomous government of the Balearic Isles.

Museu de Mallorca ★

Housed in a 17th-century mansion on Carrer de Portella, the museum exhibits archaeological remains and fine arts. Artefacts from Muslim cultures, carvings from Mallorcan churches and a fine collection of Gothic paintings are on display, as well as exhibitions of work by modern-day local artists. Open 10:00–13:00 and 16:00–18:00 October–March; 10:00–14:00 and 17:00–20:00 April–September; 10:00–14:00 Sunday; closed Monday.

Banys Arabs ★

The remains of the old Arab Baths in Carrer Serra are over a thousand years old and are one of the few examples of Moorish architecture in the city. A collection of columns and horseshoe arches, believed to be 'borrowed' from other buildings, support a domed ceiling. There are two chambers, one for reclining in the hot steam (produced by underfloor heating) and a second for cooling off. Open 09:30–20:00 April–November; 09:30–19:00 December–March.

Below: *The asymmetrical horseshoe arches of the Banys Arabs, one of the few extant examples of Moorish architecture in La Palma.*

Above: *The elegant Gothic cloisters of the Convent de Sant Francesc.*

Palau Vivot *

This superb 18th-century mansion in Carrer Zavella is not open to the public but is worth a detour just to admire its imposing courtyard, which you can see through the gates.

Convent de Sant Francesc *

Located on the Plaça Sant Francesc, on the site of an old Moorish soap factory, this is still a working monastery. Visitors enter through the cloisters, a cool oasis of lemon trees surrounded by slim Gothic pillars. The tomb of the great Mallorcan hero and polymath Ramón Llull lies behind the altar of the first chapel on the left of the main church. Outside is a statue of Mallorca's other great hero, Fra Junípero Serra, who founded the first missions of California in the 18th century (*see* p. 110).

Baratillo ***

Palma's Saturday morning flea market on Avinguda Gabriel Alomar y Villalonga is a big attraction, provided you approach with an open mind. Junk abounds and everything from household cast-offs to artificial pearls from Manacor is on sale. There's plenty of local and imported colour – just beware of con-artists and pickpockets.

Mercat Olivar *

The food market, under cover on the Plaça del Olivar, is a colourful array of fruit, vegetables, meat and fish. Gourmets will enjoy the offerings of wild mushrooms in season. Arrive early for the best of the fish.

Shopping **

The city's best shops line the Avinguda del Rei Jaume III. It is best reached from the Es Born via the Plaça Weyler and then west into the Plaça Pio XII. Where the Plaça meets the Avinguda stands a large C&A store, selling British-made clothes. The Avinguda is also known for its

ENGLISH LANGUAGE MEDIA

Recommended local English language publications include the *Mallorca Daily Bulletin*, the bi-monthly *Mallorca Tourist Info*, *The Reader* (weekly newspaper) and the glossy, Spanish and English weekly magazine, *Balearic Leisure and Living*. Foreign newspapers and magazines can be bought in the city centre and especially along the Passeig d'es Born.

fashion and jewellery shops that carry the most exquisite goods from all over the world.

Souvenirs from Mallorca range from the tasteful to the tacky but some locally-made items are a genuinely good buy, particularly embroidered linen tablecloths which are of exceptional quality, pearls from Manacor and shoes and leather goods from Inca. There's a good craft market in Plaça Major on Fridays and Saturdays. Markets are really the only place where it is acceptable to bargain, and then not too aggressively. Overseas visitors can claim back Spanish sales tax (IVA); ask the shopkeeper for a form and present it to the IVA refund office at the airport.

Poble Espanyol ★★

Spend the day wandering around this cleverly designed theme park on the western outskirts of Palma, devoted to all of Spain's varied architectural and social traditions. Attractions include lovingly crafted reproductions of the Alhambra Palace in Granada, the Giralda Tower in Sevilla and the beautiful old buildings of Toledo. You can also buy good value souvenirs from the many craft shops and there are often folk dancing displays going on, as well as the occasional food or wine promotion. Open 09:00–18:30 December–March; 09:00–20:00 April–November; closed Sundays and holidays.

Castell de Bellver ★★ (Bellver Castle)

High on a hill to the west of Palma, this great circular castle dominates the whole area. Building began in 1309 and, although the castle was originally used as a summer residence for Mallorcan kings, its main use has been as a political prison. Some inmates scratched their names on the Tower of Homage while awaiting execution. Take a taxi up and walk down through the stately pinewoods – the path begins opposite the castle entrance. Open 08:00–19:15 October–March; 08:00–20:30 April–September; 10:00–17:00 Sundays and holidays.

Below: *Castell de Bellver, an impressive 14th-century castle with grim secrets.*

Palma at a Glance

BEST TIMES TO VISIT

The best times to visit Palma are in **spring**, early **summer** and **autumn**, when there is plenty of sunshine and pleasant temperatures. The main summer months can be rather hot and the nearby resorts extremely crowded. Winters are mild.

GETTING THERE

There is an almost embarrassingly wide choice of flights, but you might need to book well in advance during the high season. **Son Sant Joan airport** is 8km (5 miles) east of Palma. Tourist information is found in the Arrivals Lounge in Terminal B. With the vast summer influx, flight delays can be frequent. *Retrasado* means 'delayed' and *embarcando* means 'boarding'. The number 17 bus leaves every 30 minutes from the airport directly to the Plaça d'Espanya in Palma. A good alternative can be to fly to Barcelona or Valencia and take the daily (car) **ferries** from there (a 9-hour, overnight trip), run by Transmediterránea.

GETTING AROUND

Renting a **car** is the best way of seeing the entire island. Make prior arrangements if you want to collect from the airport or need a child safety seat. You need to be over 21 and to have held a full licence for over six months. Do take

out fully comprehensive insurance – otherwise, if you have an accident, you might be delayed by the police. Front seat-belts are compulsory. If you meet a coach on a mountain road you are obliged to reverse. The **bus** system is extremely good; the main terminus is at **Plaça d'Espanya**. Passengers pay as they enter – always keep your ticket in case an inspector gets on. Palma buses are run by EMT (tel: 971 29 08 55), who also run a special service for the disabled (tel: 971 29 57 00). **Horse-drawn carriages**, or *tartanas*, are a traditional (and expensive) way of seeing the sights. Hire one from the Passeig de Sagrera or outside La Seu. Find out how much it will cost before you set off; the driver will expect a tip.

WHERE TO STAY

There's plenty of choice of accommodation in Palma but it's essential to book in advance if you're going to be in the city during the high season (Easter week and July–Sept). As a good and less expensive option, consider renting a holiday apartment in one of the nearby resorts.

LUXURY
Meliá Victoria, Avda. Joan Miró, tel: 971 73 25 42, fax: 971 45 08 24. Top-notch hotel with good sea views

and excellent facilities, including indoor and outdoor swimming pool, sauna, gym and shops.
Son Vida, Urb. Son Vida, tel: 971 79 00 00, fax: 971 79 00 17. Superb *gran luxe* former 13th-century castle, which is now one of Spain's top hotels. Located 8km (5 miles) out of town; facilities include swimming pool, gym, tennis; close to golf course.
Hotel San Lorenzo, c/Sant Llorenç 14, tel: 971 72 82 00; fax: 971 71 19 01. Historic Mallorcan manor house with traditional features. Picturesque garden with swimming pool.
Valparaiso Palace, c/Francisco Vidal, tel: 971 40 04 11, fax: 971 40 59 04. One of the best hotels in the city, with a panoramic view of the harbour. Good restaurant; facilities include indoor pool, solarium, mini-golf.

MID-RANGE
Mirador, Avda. Gabriel Roca 10, tel: 971 23 40 46. Quiet, traditional hotel with fine views of cathedral and waterfront.
Residencia Almudaina, Avda. Jaume III 9; tel: 971 72 73 40, fax: 971 72 25 99. A modern, and comfortable hotel in a central location.
Saratoga, Pg. Mallorca 6, tel: 971 72 72 40, fax: 971 72 73 12. Modern hotel with rooftop swimming pool.

Palma at a Glance

BUDGET

Hostal Apuntadors, c/Apuntadors 8, tel: 971 21 59 10. Cheap, good quality accommodation.

Hostal Borne, c/Sant Jaume 3, tel: 971 71 29 42. Popular, reasonably priced rooms, courtyard café.

Hostal Goya, c/Estanc 7, tel: 971 72 69 86. Cheap, basic accommodation just off the Passeig d'es Born.

Archiduque, c/Archiduque Luis Salvador 22, tel: 971 75 16 45. Atmospheric old mansion near the bus station; dogs allowed.

WHERE TO EAT

There is a wide choice of places to eat in Palma, with some of the lowest prices in the Balearics. The area around Carrer de Apuntadors offers a good selection of eating establishments. Note that restaurant opening times and days off can be moveable feasts but at least they stay open year-round.

Asador Tierra Aranda, Concepció 4, off Avda. Jaume III, tel: 971 71 42 56. Situated in an old mansion, this expensive, high-class restaurant features meaty Castilian specialities.

Bon Lloc, c/Sant Feliu 7, tel: 971 71 86 17. Relaxed atmosphere and vegetarian food at low prices.

Caballito del Mar, Pg. Sagrera, tel: 971 72 10 74. Close to Sa Llotja, with a terrace; excellent seafood.

Casa Eduardo, Industria Pequera, tel: 971 72 11 82. Busy, noisy seafood restaurant overlooking the harbour.

Cellar Sa Premsa, Bisbe Berengues de Palou 8, tel: 971 72 35 29. Hugely popular, reasonably priced seafood restaurant.

Porto Pi, Avda. Joan Miró 174, tel: 971 40 00 87. Michelin star-rated restaurant, one of Palma's best. Imaginative but expensive gourmet food.

La Zamorama, c/Apuntadors 14, no telephone. One of several cheap *tapas* bars.

SHOPPING

Shopping is easy, with supermarkets and traditional markets abounding. Shops and supermarkets open from 09:00–13:00 and 16:00–19:00, Saturday is a half-day and most shops will close on Sunday and public holidays. Mallorca is especially good for clothes shopping – the word *rebaja* means 'sale'.

TOURS AND EXCURSIONS

The most popular destinations are **Deià**, **Sóller**, **Valdemossa**, **Sa Calobra**, **Drac** (for the caves) and **Manacor** (for the pearl factories). Your hotel or the local tourist office will be able to give you details of organised tours. If you can, rent a car or take the bus or train: everywhere in Mallorca is easily reached and it's often better value for money.

USEFUL CONTACTS

Tourist Offices
There are three tourist offices in Palma; the main one is at Avda. Jaume III 10, tel: 971 71 22 16.
Central Post Office: c/de la Constitució 5, tel: 971 72 10 95.
Car rental: Betacar, Pg. Maritim 20, tel: 971 45 51 11; Avis, Pg. Maritim 19, tel: 971 73 07 20.
Airport, tel: 971 26 46 66.
Hospital Son Dureta, Andrea Doria, Palma, tel: 971 28 91 00.
Cruceros Iberia, Moll Vell 6G, tel: 971 71 71 90 for charter and boat excursions.
Transmediterránea, tel: 971 72 67 40.
Taxis Palma, tel: 971 40 14 14.
Mallorca Tennis Club, tel: 971 23 81 73.
Balearic Golf Federation, tel: 971 72 27 53.
Balearic Sailing Federation, tel: 971 40 24 12.

PALMA	J	F	M	A	M	J	J	A	S	O	N	D
AVERAGE TEMP. °C	10	9	13	14	18	22	24	24	23	18	14	12
AVERAGE TEMP. °F	50	48	54	57	64	72	76	75	73	64	58	54
HOURS OF SUN DAILY	5	6	6	7	10	11	9	11	8	6	6	4
RAINFALL mm	39	37	36	32	27	10	4	25	56	65	54	38
RAINFALL IN	1.5	1.4	1.4	1.3	1.1	0.4	0.2	1.0	2.2	2.6	2.1	1.5
DAYS OF RAINFALL	8	7	8	6	5	3	1	3	6	10	8	7

3
West of Palma

The highly developed western side of the Badia de Palma incorporates extremes of Mallorcan tourism, from the King of Spain's summer palace and row upon row of gleaming yachts to the crowded bars and beaches that typify the European package holiday destination.

To the west of the city the elegant promenade of **Cala Major** is lined with expensive looking marinas, luxury hotels and impressive private mansions, including the royal palace. Beyond here are the lively (and much maligned) resorts of **Palma Nova** and **Magaluf**, backing on to the wooded foothills of the Serra de Tramuntana.

All the main resorts as far as Palma Nova are spread along the main C719 road, although a motorway running behind the built-up area has taken considerable pressure off the residential areas. Behind the motorway, pine-scented hills lead up to the high Serra de Tramuntana. Magaluf, which virtually blends into Palma Nova, lies on the pretty **Cala Figuera** peninsula, a series of rocky bays leading down to a lookout point. Historic **Santa Ponça** – Jaume I of Aragón's beachhead in 1229 – and **Peguera**, villages on the other side of the headland, are less developed than their neighbours to the east but still get packed out in peak season.

Life on this part of the coast is dedicated to fun and sun worshipping, with countless amusement parks, excellent sailing and watersports facilities, as well as the island's impressive casino and cabaret complex. The beautiful, rugged west coast and mountains, however, are within easy driving distance.

MENORCA

Ciutadella

Santa Margalida

Artà

Porto Cristo

PALMA DE MALLORCA

MALLORCA

CLIMATE

The exposed peninsula experiences breezy weather, which can be refreshing in the height of summer and provides some excellent sailing weather. However, winter breezes are often rather chilly. Temperatures average 32°C (90°F) in July.

Opposite: *Pleasure boats cruise through the aquamarine waters of Santa Ponça Bay.*

Right: *Cala Major, long a popular holiday centre and where the Spanish royal family has a summer home.*
Opposite: *Performing dolphins entertain the crowds at Marineland.*

DON'T MISS

*** Fundació Pilar i Joan Miró: with more than 5000 exhibits.
*** Nightlife: fast, furious and fun.
** Celebrity spotting: at the luxury marina of Portals Nous, part of Mallorca's Golden Mile.
** Pretty coastal scenery: around Cala Portals Vells.
** Marineland: award-winning conservation project.

CALA MAJOR

Immediately west of Palma, this elegant sweep of hotels is rapidly subsuming neighbouring **Sant Agustí** and **Ses Illetes** (named after three small islets just offshore). The Spanish royal family have a holiday home just outside Cala Major called the **Marivent Palace**, emphasising that exclusivity can coexist with mass tourism. In fact the area was popular long before the package tour; at Illetes beach there are several small, almost old-world hotels, some so close to the beach you can sleep and wake to the sound of breaking surf.

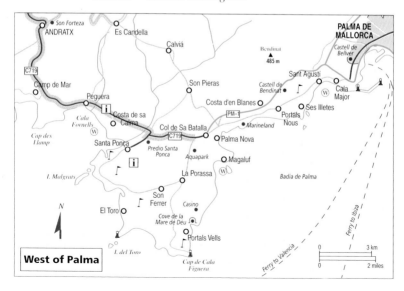

West of Palma

Fundació Pilar i Joan Miró ★★★

In Cala Major some 4km (2 ½miles) from Palma (bus number 21 from the Plaça d'Espanya in Palma), over 5000 of world-renowned Joan Miró's artworks are housed in a series of purpose-built galleries that reflect the landscape he loved so much. Miró adored his own land and never ceased to find inspiration in its colours, shapes and traditions. A trip to the Fundació is recommended as much for the insights into the Spanish, and Mallorcan characters, as for the artworks themselves, superb though they might be. Open 10:00–19:00 Tuesday–Saturday (10:00–18:00 winter); Sunday 10:00–15:00 (11:00–13:00 winter).

THE GOLDEN MILE
Portals Nous ★★

West of Cala Major, the coastline has fast become known as the Golden Mile, the upmarket area of **Bendinat** merging into a very smart marina at **Port Punta Portals**, carved out of the rocky shoreline. The marina plays host to many of the world's finest yachts and is a good place to people-watch at sunset or to enjoy a long, lazy lunch. There's a pleasant beach at Portals Nous, backed by feathery pines with some rocky areas for sunbathing.

Marineland ★★

Some 3km (2 miles) further west brings you to **Costa d'en Blanes**, with its award-winning Marineland dolphinarium. As well as putting on shows for children, Marineland runs a conservation project for Patagonian and Californian sealions and breeds endangered species, including turtles and macaws. Open 09:30–19:30 daily (18:00 winter).

BENDINAT

The resort area of Bendinat, spread around an old manor estate, is supposed to have got its name from Jaume I of Aragón who, on a visit in September 1229, claimed '*bé havem dinat*', Catalan for 'we have dined well'. The king must have been easily pleased – all he had consumed was bread and garlic. An air of prestige was nonetheless bestowed on the area and today it boasts an 18th-century castle and a golf course, **Real Golf de Bendinat**, as well as holiday villas shaded by pine trees.

Palma Nova

Palma Nova and its neighbour, Magaluf, received a lot of bad publicity in the 1980s as sub-standard, even violent tourist ghettos frequented by British 'lager louts'. A massive security clampdown by the Mallorcan authorities has improved the behaviour of the clientele and the most offensive of the 1960s-style concrete blocks have been pulled down and replaced with more attractive low-rise buildings and palm trees.

Today, both resorts offer harmless, action-packed fun, bursting with fast food establishments, enormous bars serving beer from around the world, and wall-to-wall souvenir shops. Discos thud until dawn and in summer the streets are packed with young holidaymakers who do little more than toast themselves on the warm sand during the day and dance through the night.

Golf Fantasia *

A very brief walk inland from Palma Nova brings you to Golf Fantasia, a fairly advanced crazy golf course. Natural and unnatural hazards ranging from tropical jungles to waterfalls and caves provide hours of entertainment for all the family. Open 10:30–24:00 daily.

Magaluf

Magaluf is a good, if highly developed, resort for families, with plenty of attractions for children. **Aquapark**, on the road south to Portals Vells and Cala Figuera, is highly rated. Take a dive in Nemo, a working submarine, add to this go-carting, riding, tennis and all types of water sports, and it's easy to understand why this area has retained its popularity. The beaches are sandy and good while nearby pinewoods offer sweet-scented seclusion for those who feel the occasional need to be alone.

CALA PORTALS VELLS

Here is one of the miracles of Mallorca: how quickly noisy, exuberant areas change to places of relative peace and tranquility within a scant few miles. Following the signs south from Magaluf for Portals Vells and Cala Figuera, the road leads through pinewoods, past a well designed golf course and a left hand turn-off to **Platja Mago** (a discreet nudist beach) until you arrive at an entrancing bay called Cala Portals Vells. The bay can, however, get extremely busy in the summer months.

Above: *Young holidaymakers flock to Magaluf for its superb beach and exuberant nightlife.*
Opposite: *Calm seas and sandy beaches are some of Palma Nova's attractions.*

Cove de la Mare de Déu *

A few hundred metres along the bay, accessible only on foot – or by boat from Magaluf – is the Cove de la Mare de Déu. Here a small chapel has been carved from sold rock, a shrine supposedly dating from the Middle Ages, when Genoese sailors erected a statue of the Virgin Mary in a small cave as a 'thank you' for being saved from shipwreck. Stone from the area was also used in the building of Palma's La Seu Cathedral.

Cala Figuera **

This is a small resort specialising in self-catering holidays, with apartments and houses shaded by the trees. La Figuera itself is the southernmost tip of Mallorca, a small

---

TOURIST NUMBER ONE

King Juan Carlos and Queen Sophia, their children Elena, Christina and Felipe have been holidaying on Mallorca for years. Known affectionately, as *los Reyes*, or 'the Royals', the King jokingly refers to himself as Tourist Number One. No question but that their presence has helped make Mallorca as fashionable with the jet set as it is with the package tourist.

Above: *The peaceful, picturesque cove of Cala Fornells.*

peninsula used by the military, so access is restricted. However, there are more than enough tiny coves and beaches around Portals Vells for visitors to relax in comparative solitude.

Santa Ponça **

Some 19km (12 miles) from Palma, on the western side of the Cala Figuera peninsula, is one of the finest sandy beaches on the island, its azure waters shallow and safe for children. Out at sea, however, there's usually a massed flotilla of swimmers, windsurfers, water-skiers and speed-boats. The town becomes extremely crowded during the high season; spring and early autumn are probably the best times to stay. There's an 18-hole golf course nearby and good scuba diving around the coast. The resort is also historically important: Jaume I landed here in 1229 and began to take back the island from the Moors. Near the marina is a superb viewpoint, the Caleta de Santa Ponça, where a white cross on the headland commemorates Jaume I's landing.

Peguera *

West of Santa Ponça, Peguera is one of the better package tour destinations on Mallorca. It has a relaxed air, despite the inevitable summer crowds, partly due to the new by-pass that swings the main road around to the north, partly due to long-term residents quietly determined to preserve their own version of paradise – a sandy beach lined with pine trees. It is a place to relax and sip wine, enjoying the view from your balcony or terrace. Nearby, **Cala Fornells** is the place from where to see spectacular sunsets.

CATALUNYA'S GOLDEN AGE

From the 12th century to the 14th, Catalunya ruled an empire that included Sicily, Malta, Sardinia, most of modern Greece, the Balearics and parts of southern France. Catalunya's greatest ruler was Jaume I, the king responsible for the reconquest of Mallorca in 1229.

West of Palma at a Glance

BEST TIMES TO VISIT

The best times to visit are in early **spring** or **autumn**. Winter is mild but many hotels are closed. The hinterland is peaceful all year round and you can find the odd semi-deserted beach.

GETTING THERE

The western resorts all lie near Palma. The **roads** are good, though crowded, with regular **bus services** from the Plaça d'Espanya in Palma.

GETTING AROUND

Most visitors to this area are package tourists and tend not to stray from their resort. If you'd like to go further afield hire a **car** or take the **bus**.

WHERE TO STAY

Hotels and apartments cater for package holidays and are booked solid by tour operators. Prices are higher than other parts of the island. Many hotels close for winter.

LUXURY

Bon Sol, Pg. Illetes 30, Ses Illetes, tel: 971 40 21 11, fax: 971 40 25 59. Family-run hotel with a secluded beach. Near golf course.
Meliá de Mar, Pg. Illetes 7, Ses Illetes, tel: 971 40 25 11, fax: 971 40 58 52. One of the most luxurious and elegant on the island. Large pool and wonderful gardens.
Villamil, Avda. Peguera, Peguera, tel: 971 68 60 50,

fax: 971 68 68 15. Sophisticated hotel; sun terraces, tennis court.

MID-RANGE

Hotel Bendinat, Avda. Bendinat 58, Bendinat; tel: 971 67 57 25, fax: 971 67 72 76. Small, traditional Mallorcan hotel.
Beverley Playa, Urb. La Romana, Peguera, tel: 971 68 60 70, fax: 971 68 61 20. Close to beach and pinewoods. Reasonably priced; excellent facilities.
Sol Antillas, Violeta 1, Magaluf, tel: 971 13 15 00, fax: 971 13 02 05. Popular package tour venue, close to beach. Heated pool and full entertainment programme.

BUDGET

Bon Repós, Via Rei Sancho 8, Santa Ponça, tel: 971 69 03 66. Medium-sized hotel with pleasant bar and terrace.
Mimosa, c/Sueca 5, Sant Augusti. Good value bed and breakfast.
Gil, Rosés Bermejo 24, Palma Nova, tel: 971 68 10 40. Small pleasant budget hotel.

WHERE TO EAT

The home of international cuisine and fast-food country, there are restuarants specialising in Mallorcan food.
Bon Aire d'Illetes, Avda. Adelfas, Ses Illetes, tel: 971 40 00 48. Expensive Spanish/Mallorcan and international dishes.

Can Jaume, c/Cala Figuera, Magaluf, tel: 971 68 03 82. Rural Mallorcan cooking.
Ciro's, Pg. del Mar, Palma Nova, tel 971 68 10 52. Pleasant, quiet restaurant with a terrace; Mediterranean cuisine.
Sa Masia, c/Andratx, Santa Ponça, tel: 971 69 42 17. Expensive imaginative menu – try the *espinagada*.
Tristán, Port Punta Portals, Portals Nous, tel: 971 67 55 47. Smart, fashionable Michelin-rated restaurant at the marina; good nouvelle cuisine.

TOURS AND EXCURSIONS

Full-day and half-day coach tours go from the resorts to **Deià**, **Sóller**, **Valldemossa** and **Sa Colobra** on the western coast. Details at hotels or the local tourist office. The casino at Calvià has regular flamenco shows from May–October, tel: 971 45 45 08.

Sports

There are 18-hole golf courses at Poniente (Magaluf), Santa Ponça and Bendinat. The resorts have excellent facilities, particularly for watersports.

USEFUL CONTACTS

Tourist Offices
Palma Nova: Pg. del Mar, tel: 971 68 23 65.
Magaluf: Avda. Magaluf, 20, tel: 971 13 11 26; fax: 971 13 11 26.
Santa Ponça: Puig de Galatzó, tel: 971 69 17 12.

4
The West Coast

Mallorca's western region is geographically quite different from the rest of the island, comprising the **Serra de Tramuntana** mountain range, which falls away into the sea on one side and flattens out onto the island's central plain on the other. The coastline is especially loved by walkers, for it offers a rare opportunity to find total solitude amidst spectacular scenery. Twisting mountain paths reveal tantalising glimpses of hidden bays, the water an iridescent shade of turquoise, a lone yacht sometimes anchored for a picnic lunch. Feathery pine trees scent the air and, in spring, the mountains are carpeted with wildflowers.

The area also includes several of the island's main cultural attractions, the light and beauty of the mountains having attracted artists, mystics and hermits for years. Poet Robert Graves is buried in **Deià** and the composer Frédérick Chopin lived in **Valldemossa**. Visit the craft centre at **Sa Granja**, west of Valldemossa, and the Carthusian monastery where Chopin lived. Further north, **Sóller** is a fascinating town connected by an old electric railway to Palma; the restored Moorish house and gardens of **Alfabia** are close by.

Take time to explore the mountains. The coast road is beautiful but painfully slow and winding and even the main road from Palma north to Sóller has some amazing hairpins as it crosses the high peaks. Cycling, walking or meandering from one village to the next is a better way to enjoy the area than trying to do everything in one day; the scenery is at its best early in the morning or at dusk.

CLIMATE

Slightly cooler than the rest of the island, the summers are pleasantly relaxing, with temperatures of around 29°C (84°F), and the odd cloud is not unusual. The mountains act as a rainshadow, with a build-up of cloud cover and higher rainfall than the rest of the island.

Opposite: *Mallorca's mountainous west coast is dotted with charming old villages.*

DON'T MISS

*** Deià: beautiful artists'
colony also favoured by the
international jet set.
*** Monasteri de Lluc:
Mallorca's spiritual centre.
*** Sa Calobra: a
spectacular mountain road
twisting downwards to an
exquisite rugged cove.
*** Valldemossa: winter
love-nest of famous 19th-
century Romantics.
* Torrent de Pareis:
breathtaking canyon scenery.

THE ISLAND'S WESTERN TIP

Some 25km (15 miles) west of Palma along the C179 is
Camp de Mar. This is a popular cove, where every
square inch of steeply sloping shoreline appears to have
been developed, but without appearing crass. It is as if
the buildings help land and sea merge into one and at
night, when the water reflects the myriad lights, it's hard
to see where the one begins and the other ends. From
here you can walk through pine trees and up into a
heather-covered headland, then down into Port
d'Andratx. You can drive too, but the walk is especially
beautiful in the evening or early morning.

Port d'Andratx *

A long-time favourite haunt of the yachting fraternity,
this upmarket resort has a lovely natural harbour.
There's still plenty of traditional charm, good – but
expensive – restaurants and fishing village atmosphere
around the harbour's south side.

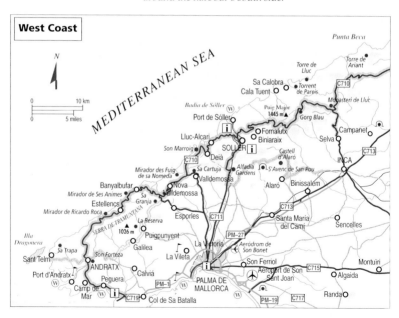

Andratx itself is some 5km (3 miles) inland from its port – typical of many Mallorcan villages, which were built back from the sea to avoid pirate attacks. Approached through orange groves, Andratx presents an air of solemnity and purpose, helped by its tall houses and the imposing 13th-century church of Santa María. Close by is a former Moorish fort, converted in the 16th century to a Mallorcan mansion known as **Son Mas**. The view from here, over the surrounding orange groves and down to Port d'Andratx, is spectacular.

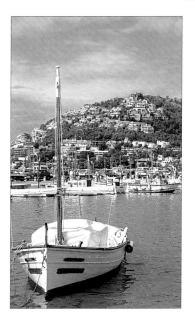

Above: *Expensive yachts fill the harbour at exclusive Port d'Andratx.*

Sant Telm and Sa Dragonera **

From Andratx, drive the 8km (5 miles) due west to the one-time sleepy fishing port of Sant Telm. From here you can take a boat trip around the off-shore island of Sa Dragonera, now a nature reserve despite demands for it to be developed for tourism. Landing is forbidden unless prior permission has been obtained, and then will only be granted to accredited naturalists.

However, Sant Telm is perhaps more notable as the gateway to **Sa Trapa**, a ruined but romantic clifftop Trappist monastery. It can be reached by the monk's original track, steep and a little scary in places, or by a rough inland road developed by the volunteers who are busy restoring the original buildings.

Galilea and Puigpunyent *

Inland from Andratx, a precarious mountain road twists its way north to the villages of Galilea and Puigpunyent. The countryside is a welcome, green break from the coast and in spring and early summer it's alive with almond and orange blossom. Galilea has now become something of an artist's colony, but is less fashionable than Deià. From the parish church in Plaça Pío XII there are spectacular views of the coast. Puigpunyent, some 8km (5 miles) further on, leads to La Reserva.

> ### SA DRAGONERA
>
> In 1977, protesters against the rampant commercialisation of Mallorca's southern coast occupied the island of Sa Dragonera. Today it is an exclusive nature reserve, but touring its shores still makes for a pleasant boat ride, while bird-watchers can rejoice in all the varied gulls to be seen, and might even spot an Eleanora's falcon.

Above: *The old Moorish palace of Sa Granja is now a 'living' museum.*
Opposite: *Lovely old Valldemossa, birthplace of Mallorca's only saint.*

MIRADORES

Miradores, now view points, were originally watch-towers against the permanent threat of invasion from the sea. Look for the **Mirador de Ses Animes**, on the Estellencs/Banyalbufar road where the watchtower has been restored, or past the village of Estellencs where the **Mirador Coll des Pi** has a café and a service station. The **Mirador de Ricardo Roca** has a restaurant and a remarkable view.

La Reserva ★★

Nestling on the slopes of the Puig de Galatzó, this is a privately owned nature reserve of some 20,000ha (49,420 acres). A well marked trail takes you through woods dotted with waterfalls and caves, past a reconstructed charcoal burner's hut and ancient gnarled olive trees. Creatures from birds of prey to brown bears inhabit the reserve. The walk takes about 90 minutes but, despite handrails on the steepest parts, is not suitable for the infirm. There is an adventure circuit including abseiling, rope bridges and climbing for the more active. Open 10:00–sunset, daily.

Sa Granja ★★★

North of Puigpunyent is Sa Granja, once a Moorish palace, then a Cistercian monastery. Today it is a privately owned 'living museum' dedicated to preserving Mallorcan arts and crafts. Museum staff – some in traditional costume – demonstrate how wool is spun, lace, candles and cheese made and bread baked, much as they were centuries ago. An old-fashioned pharmacy makes medicines from the hundreds of plants grown in Sa Granja's extensive gardens. There are regular folk dancing displays; visitors can also enjoy local wines and home-made liqueurs. Open 10:00–19:00 (10:00–18:00 winter).

Banyalbufar ★

This picturesque town northwest of Sa Granja was once an old Moorish village, whose name in Arabic means 'little vineyard by the sea'. The hills behind the town were terraced by the Moors, and they are still mostly worked by hand, with tomatoes being the main produce.

So steep is the slope on which the village is built that many of the houses are supported by stilts. With few hotels or amenities, tourism hasn't made much of an impact here and Banyabulfar is as discrete and out of the way as anywhere in Mallorca.

VALLDEMOSSA

This charming town owes its main claim to fame to the visit paid by French novelist George Sand and Frédérick Chopin, the Polish composer, who stayed here in the winter of 1838–9. Today coachloads of tourists flock to see the couple's lodgings in the beautiful old Carthusian monastery, the Sa Cartuja.

Sa Cartuja ★★★

Also known as **Reial Cartoixa**, the monastery is comprised mainly of 18th-century buildings in a picturesque, mountainous setting. Visitors have occasionally – and mistakenly – assumed that the monks lived in some luxury. Each so-called 'cell' has its own living room, tiny chapel and private garden. In fact, the Carthusian monks were more like individual hermits. Each monk was expected to be as self-sufficent as possible and contact between them was minimal.

After the monks' expulsion in 1835, the cells were sold off. Chopin and George Sand were some of the first to stay in the newly privatised rooms. Cells said to have been used by the couple have been transformed into a museum

---

CHOPIN AND SAND

Composer Frédérick Chopin and his lover, the French authoress George Sand, spent the winter of 1838–9 in Mallorca, living in three of the abandoned monk's cells of the old Carthusian monastery at Valldemossa. They had been forced to leave their villa in nearby Establiments when the villagers discovered Chopin suffered from tuberculosis, for the disease was known to be contagious. Equally, the villagers objected to George Sand who wore trousers and smoked cigarettes in the street, and never bothered to disguise her contempt for people she described as being like monkeys or Polynesian cannibals. Her book, *Un Hiver en Mallorque*, paints a fairly dismal picture of life on the island.

dedicated to them. Memorabilia includes George Sand's original manuscript of *Un hiver en Mallorque* and two pianos that belonged to Chopin, along with original music scores and his death-mask. Piano recitals are held hourly in summer.

Another highlight of the monastery is the **Prior's Cell**, which has a fascinating library of rare books. There's also an enormous church with frescoes by Goya's brother-in-law, Manuel Bayeu, and an 18th-century pharmacy. A Chopin music festival is held in the monastery during the summer; tel: (971) 612351 for further information. Open 09:30–18:00 March–October; 09:30–16:00 November–February; 10:00–13:00 Sunday.

Costa Nord *

Actor Michael Douglas endorses a small exhibition of the north coast, its people and traditions. A short film, a recreation of the interior of Archduke Ludwig Salvador of Austria's ship and the Tramuntana mountain range exhibition are open from 09:00–19:00 daily.

Palau del Rei Sanc *

Built as a hunting lodge in the 14th century for King Sancho, this was the original Carthusian monastery and is adjacent to Sa Cartuja. Folk dancing displays are held every Monday and Thursday morning in the summer. Open 09:30–13:00; 15:00–18:30 Monday–Saturday.

Valldemossa was the birthplace of Mallorca's only saint, Santa Catalina Tomás, in 1531. Santa Catalina impressed with her devotion and goodness rather than miracles. She is revered throughout the entire island, but

---

TAPAS

A selection of *tapas* makes a good substitute for a meal for travellers on a budget. Originally *tapas*, meaning 'lids', were little plates placed on top of the glass when a drink was served, bearing a free snack. *Tapas* are not a Mallorcan speciality but most bars serve them. Free snacks today are found only in local bars, far from the tourist haunts and it is more common to display the dishes of the day at the bar and sell small portions for very low prices. Look out for *boquerones* (deep fried anchovies); *tortilla* (Spanish omelette), served cold); meatballs; *sobrasada* (sausages); potato salad and marinated squid.

in Valldemossa it is rare to find a house without a coloured tile on its wall that asks for Santa Catalina's intercession. The house where she was born in the Carrer de Rectoria is now a shrine.

Son Marroig ★★

The road north from Valldemossa, the C710, leads past the impressive mansion and grounds of Son Marroig, once the home of Archduke Ludwig Salvador of Austria (1847–1915). Ludwig visited Mallorca in 1876 and returned in 1878 – this time to stay until his death.

A confirmed mallorcophile, the archduke was a philanthropist and enthusiastic dilettante with a wide range of interests. He gave generous financial support to projects concerned with discovering and preserving Mallorca's heritage, and is venerated on the island. Today Son Marroig is a museum packed with Ludwig's memorabilia, including Mallorcan furniture and ceramics, paintings, photographs and books. There are sensational panoramic views from the beautiful gardens. Open 9:30–14:00; 16:30–20:00 Monday –Saturday (18:00 winter).

Deia

Son Marroig lies just outside Deià, a town best known as the home of Robert Graves, buried in the local graveyard with the single word epitaph: *poeta*. Beautiful, but notorious for its weather, its fair share of rain is a small price to pay for its position. Pretty houses and steep, cobbled streets leading into orange and lemon groves, while olive trees stand on the surrounding terraces. Yet even as Deià has retained its charm and easy-going approach to life, passing jet-set visitors, attracted to the acclaimed hotel **La Residencia**, have helped push prices up. Pretty as it is, Deià can be very expensive.

Opposite: *One of the tranquil private gardens belonging to Sa Cartuja's invidual cells.*
Below: *Deià, a picturesque Mallorcan town long favoured by expatriate writers and artists.*

Port de Sóller ★★

The C710 leads further north to Lluc-Alcari, with three watch towers and a mirador providing yet more splendid views, especially over the circular bay of Port de Sóller. The name comes from the Arabic word *sulltar*, meaning 'golden shell', so struck were the Moors by the natural beauty of the bay and valley beyond.

Port de Sóller was, in tourist terms, originally discovered by the French. It has an air of restrained elegance and is very reminiscent of the south of France. You can swim from a small sandy beach south of the Badia de Sóller, or take a boat trip to **Sa Calobra** further north along the coast. There is also a pleasant walk to the lighthouse, **Faro de Punta Grossa**, through the woods, past villas owned by the wealthy and on to hills covered in euphorbia, pines and wild rosemary. The more energetic might like to continue to Punta de Sóller on the cliffs southwest of the lighthouse, from where you can see **Lluc-Alcari** and **Cap Gros**. You will have to scramble across a river to get there, but the view – and often, the solitude – are both well worth it.

Right: *Nets drying on the quayside lend elegant Port de Sóller a touch of authentic fishing village charm.*
Opposite: *Visitors relax in an open-air cafe in tranquil Sóller.*

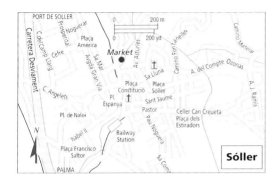

Sóller

SOLLER

The town of Sóller, situated in the Valle de los Naranjos, is surrounded by orange, lemon and almond groves and kept temperate by Mallorca's tallest mountain, the 1445m (4740ft) **Puig Major**. Its buildings are of traditional Mallorcan design plus ideas picked up abroad. Joan Rubió, for example, studied under Antoni Gaudí – don't miss his Modernista **Banco de Sóller** and the next-door church of **Sant Bartolomeu** in the Plaça Constitució. On the Carrer de Sa Mar is the small **Museu Municipal**, with relics of the old town. Open 11:00–13:00, 16:00–19:00 Sunday–Friday. Don't miss the Museu Balear de Ciencias Naturales (Natural Science Musuem) and botanical garden. Open 10:00–20:00 April–September; 10:00–17:30 October–March; 10:30–13:30 Sundays and holidays; closed Monday.

Alfabia Gardens **

Some 9km (5 miles) south of Sóller are the Alfabia Gardens. Once owned by a Moorish lord, there's a ramshackle villa with old furniture and gardens with shaded walks, ponds and exotic trees and shrubs. Don't miss the pergola, a long walkway covered with creeping views entwined around ancient stone columns. Open 09:30–17:30 September–May; 09:30–18:30 June –August; closed Sunday and Saturday afternoon.

Biniaraix and Fornalutx ★

Two attractive mountain villages that form regular stop-offs on the tourist trail are Biniaraix and Fornalutx, on the road east from Sóller. Biniaraix is little more than a hamlet, but Fornalutx has several bars and one or two pleasant places to stay. A large proportion of Fornalutx's postcard-pretty houses are foreign-owned.

Gorg Blau ★

The road north from Sóller leads to the Gorg Blau pass, 550m (1805ft) long and 110m (328ft) deep. This picturesque spot is marked by a column, unearthed in 1969, that is thought to have belonged to a sixth-century temple. Now comes a tunnel and almost immediately after, the turn off west to Sa Calobra.

FOREST FIRES

Forest fires are a serious threat to Mallorca in summer when the undergrowth becomes dry and brittle. Visitors should observe a strict code of conduct. Never light fires in the wild if a sign forbids it, or throw away cigarette butts or leave glass objects lying around. Where campfires are permitted, put them out with water and earth and make sure there are no embers still glowing when you leave. If you see a fire, report it immediately; severe forest fires in the mountains usually have to be put out from the air.

SA CALOBRA

The road to Sa Calobra is one of the most impressive and terrifying in Europe. It snakes downwards for 14km (5 miles) in a succession of the tightest hairpins that engineers have ever constructed, yet seems mere child's play to the drivers of huge tourist coaches. But the drive alone is worth it, for the limestone cliffs have been weathered into shapes that defy description. Turrets, organ pipes, even huge faces loom large, all playing home to a profusion of Alpine plants. Finally you arrive at Sa Colobra, which used to be one of the islands best kept secrets – a perfect cove only reached by boat. Even though the world has now discovered Sa Calobra, it is still well worth a visit. There is a modern holiday development called **Cala Tuent**, a car park and several bars and restaurants clustered around the beach.

Torrent de Pareis **

Allow time to walk from Sa Calobra through a series of low-cut tunnels to Mallorca's own Grand Canyon, formed by the Torrent de Pareis, that has carried water down from the Serra de Tramuntana for millennia. The gorge is only 30m (100ft) wide, but its dimensions are enhanced by cliffs that soar vertically 600m (1000ft). The effect has been likened to falling into a crack in the earth. The Torrent de Pareis meets the Mediterranean at a warm, sandy beach, usually covered with warm, sandy bodies.

Lluc ***

Heading north on the C710, the next place of interest is the Monasteri de Lluc. Mallorca's chief pilgrimage site has been popular since the Middle Ages, thanks to its 13th-century statue of the Virgin, known as La Moreneta – the little dark one.

Today more than 50,000 pilgrims a year visit the shrine and the old Augustinian monastery. During the summer you can hear the heavenly voices of Es Blavets (the blue ones), a boys' choir named after the colour of their cassocks. Of particular interest are the eye-catching Modernista sculptures lining the route to the shrine by Antoni Gaudí and Joan Rubió.

THE BROWN MADONNA

Legend enshrouds La **Moreneta**, a small, brown statue of the Virgin Mary in the monastery at Lluc. The statue was allegedly found by a shepherd boy in the nearby forest. He took it to the parish priest, who proclaimed it as being the Virgin, placing it in the church at **Escorca**. Twice the statue vanished, always found again in the place where the shepherd boy first discovered it. Eventually the parish priest had a chapel built in the woods to honour the Brown Madonna.

Opposite: *Nerve-shattering hairpin bends snake along the mountain road to Sa Calobra.*
Left: *Lluc Monastery, important pilgrimage site and home to sculptures by Modernista master Antoni Gaudí.*

West Coast at a Glance

BEST TIME TO VISIT

Places in the mountains or in their rainshadow, like Valldemossa or Deià, can be a little wet in the winter. **Spring** is marvellous, when the almond trees are in full bloom.

GETTING THERE

The C719 coastal **road** from Palma to Andratx and Sóller, turns into the C710; otherwise take the C711 from Palma straight to Sóller. Resorts organize **coach** trips to tourist attractions. The **train** from Palma to Sóller runs through the mountains, and takes 1½ hours; tel: 971 75 20 51.

GETTING AROUND

The best way to see the west coast is by **car**; you can get around by **bus** but the service isn't particularly frequent.

WHERE TO STAY

There aren't that many high-rise hotels or purpose-built apartment blocks but there are more varied types of accommodation. Consider staying in a *finca*, a villa or converted farmhouse. Contact the Associació Agroturisme Balear, c/Foners 8, Palma, tel: 971 77 03 36, fax: 971 46 69 10 for further information. The **Monastery of Lluc** has self-contained cells with the use of a kitchen and dining room. It's jam-packed during the summer – tel: 971 51 70 25 to reserve a room. People staying at the

small hotel at the **Castell d'Alaró** are faced with a longish climb on foot – but if you call a few days ahead (971 51 04 80), you can arrange to have a donkey plus driver meet you where the mountain path begins.

Banyalbufar
LUXURY
Son Net Hotel, tel: 971 14 70 00, fax: 971 14 70 01. New luxurious country hotel with lavish gardens.
Baronia, c/General Goded 16, tel: 971 61 01 21. Comfortable country-style accommodation with good coastal views.

Deià
LUXURY
Es Molí, Ctra. Valldemossa to Deià, tel: 971 63 90 00, fax: 971 63 93 33. Lov ely old stone mansion in splendid gardens, with private beach and many facilities.
La Residencia, Finca Son Canals, Deià, tel: 971 63 90 11, fax: 971 63 93 33. Beautiful upmarket hotel, facilities include large swimming pool, garden and excellent restaurant. An overall air of relaxed luxury.

Port d'Andratx
LUXURY
Club Camp de Mar, Camp de Mar, tel: 971 10 52 00, fax: 971 10 51 10. Luxury hotel in picturesque location;

excellent facilities including many sports.

MID-RANGE
Brismar, Almirante Riera Alemany 6, tel: 971 67 16 00, fax: 971 67 11 83. A charming seafront hotel with reasonable restaurant; facilities for the disabled.

Port de Sóller
MID-RANGE
Miramar, c/Marina 12, tel: 971 63 13 50, fax: 971 63 26 71. Popular hotel with reasonably priced rooms.
Edén Park, Lepanto 2, Port de Sóller, tel: 971 63 12 00, fax: 971 63 36 56. A modern hotel conveniently situated very close to seafront.

Sóller
MID-RANGE
Espléndido, Pg. Es Trans 5, tel: 971 63 18 50, fax: 971 63 30 19. An old-fashioned and pleasant hotel with facilities for disabled visitors; pets are also welcomed.
El Guía, c/Castanyer 3, tel: 971 63 02 27, fax: 971 63 02 27. Lovely one-star hotel which also has good food.

BUDGET
Nadal, Romerguera 27, tel: 971 63 11 80. Small, central hotel with terrace.
Primavera Ctra. Puerto, tel: 971 63 40 53. Small and very friendly hotel in picturesque location.

West Coast at a Glance

Sant Telm
MID-RANGE
Aquamarín, Platja de Sant Telm, Sant Telm, tel: 971 10 91 05. It is usually busy on the weekends due to the excellent bar and restaurant.

Valldemossa
LUXURY
Vistamar, Ctra. Valldemossa to Andratx, tel: 971 61 23 00, fax: 971 61 25 83. Small, charming and exclusive countryside hotel with excellent restaurant.

MID-RANGE
Can Mário, c/Vetam 8, tel: 971 61 21 22. Small, typical Mallorcan hotel with good home cooking.

WHERE TO EAT

Most restaurants close either Monday or Tuesday, so always check in advance. If you book, do not necessarily expect to eat exactly at the time arranged.

Alfabia
Ses Porxeres, Carretera Sóller, tel: 971 61 37 62. Next to the Alfabia Gardens, which is as good a place as any to walk off a three-hour lunch.

Deià
Mirador de Na Fordador, tel: 971 63 90 26. Specializes in Mallorcan country food.
Can Quet, Crta. Deià, tel: 971 63 91 96. Popular restaurant that cooks international cusine in Mallorcan style.

El Olivo, Son Canals, Deià, tel: 971 63 90 11. Expensive Mediterranean nouvelle cuisine patronized by celebrities; come here for a special treat.

Lluc
Escorca Restaurant, on the Sóller–Lluc road, no telephone. Mountain restaurant specializing in traditional country fare.
Es Guix, Urb. Es Guix, Lluc, tel: 971 51 70 92. Lovely terrace retaurant with good Mallorcan food; swimming pool. Gets very crowded at weekends.

Port d'Andratx
Bar Lovente, next to Club Nautico, Port d'Andratx, no telephone. Seafood restaurant popular with locals and tourists alike.
El Patio, Ctra. Andratx–Port d'Andratx, tel: 971 67 20 18. Elegant with good food – the set menu is excellent value.
Layn, Almirante Niera 9, tel: 971 62 30 11. Celebrity-studded seafood restuarant overlooking the bay

Port de Sóller
Es Canyis, Passeig Platja, tel: 971 63 14 06. Seafront: serves good French-style food.

Sóller
Sa Cova d'en Jordi, Plaça Constitució 7, tel: 971 63 32 22. Clean, hospitable and with a varied menu.

Valldemossa
Can Pedro, c/Arxiduc Louis Salvador 6, tel: 971 61 21 70. Wholesome Mallorcan food.

Sant Telm
Flexus, on the seafront, no telephone. Simple restaurant with fabulous views of Sa Dragonera. Specializes in fresh fish; the grilled sardines are excellent.

TOURS AND EXCURSIONS

Mallorca's size means that it is possible to visit virtually any part of the island in a day, and many tour/excursion companies exist to enable you to do just that. Within this specific area, **La Reserva**, tel: 971 61 66 22, and **Sa Granja,** tel: 971 61 00 32, are especially recommended. It is customary to tip both the driver and the guide – and it is worth checking beforehand whether there will be an English-speaking guide.

USEFUL CONTACTS

Tourist Offices
Sóller: Plaça de Sa Constitució, 1, tel: 971 63 03 32, fax: 971 63 37 22.
Valldemossa: Sa Cartuja (Reial Cartoixa) de Valldemossa, tel: 971 61 21 06.
Aquamarine Diving, Port d'Andratx, tel: 971 67 43 76.
ICONA Pg. de Guillermo de Torrela, Palma, tel: 971 71 74 40 for information on fishing at Gorg Blau.

5
The North Coast

Mallorca's northeast coast is comprised of two vast, sandy bays, Pollença and Alcúdia, divided by the rocky Aucanada Peninsula and Cap d'es Pinar, a cape clad in pines. The northern tip of the Serra de Tramuntana juts out into the sea, forming the dramatic **Cap de Formentor**, which in turn shelters the sandy bay of **Port de Pollença**, a peaceful family resort and fishing village. The Badia de Pollença ends where the island's second, less dramatic mountain range, the Serra de Llevant, rises out of the central plain.

Alcúdia itself is an old Roman settlement with a few traces of its origins still visible. Alcúdia's port, meanwhile, is a busy, commercial base packed with naval and pleasure craft as well as fishing boats and forming the northern end of a long string of holiday developments encircling the bay.

Behind the lively scene on the coast is **S'Albufera**, a lonely stretch of marshy wetlands, home to thousands of migratory birds and popular with ornithologists. The swamps give way to drained salt pans on the central plain, covered by hundreds of windmills. The most important historical feature of this area is **Ses Païsses**, a well-preserved Bronze Age settlement near **Artà**, an attractive country town located on the Serra de Llevant.

The north coast resorts make a good base from which to explore the northern end of the Tramuntana mountains as well as the dramatic caves and pretty coves down the island's eastern side. A good main road links Alcúdia to Palma for sightseeing and access to the airport.

MENORCA

Ciutadella

Santa
Margalida

Artà

PALMA DE
MALLORCA

Porto
Cristo

MALLORCA

CLIMATE

Affording some of the best shelter from wind on the island, the Badia d'Alcúdia has summer temperatures that can reach as high as 40°C (105°F), but are more likely to be around 33°C (91°F) – still extremely hot. Breezes are non-existent and cloud cover during the summer is virtually unheard of. Not ideal for the fairskinned!

Opposite: *The spectacular craggy coastline of the Formentor Peninsula gives way to magnificent coastal views.*

Right: *Locals and visitors alike flock to Pollença's popular Sunday morning market.*
Opposite: *Mediterranean sunlight bathes the sandstone buildings of Pollença.*

Don't Miss

*** Aucanada Peninsula: spectacular coastal walks.
*** S'Albufera: fabulous, unspoilt nesting site for migrating birds.
*** Ses Païsses: Mallorca's most important Bronze Age settlement near Artà.
** Alcúdia: ancient Roman ruins and well preserved medieval town.
** Sa Colònia de Sant Pere: a near unspoilt traditional fishing village.

POLLENÇA

Despite its legendary traffic problems (use one of the car parks on the outskirts and then walk), Pollença is one of the island's favourite towns, popular with tourists and Mallorcans alike. As the road descends from the mountains, carob and oak trees begin to appear and then, without warning, you are surrounded by bright wildflowers and orchards, and the eagles and vultures that flew overhead so little time ago are replaced by song birds, doves and pigeons.

Pollença is a pretty town in a valley surrounded by the Serra de Tramuntana and the Puig de Pollença, and is bisected by a river, the Torrent de Sant Jordi, which boasts a supposedly Roman bridge. However, some experts think that the bridge was in fact built by the Moors in the 12th century, who would naturally have followed Roman techniques and design. The town's name comes from the Latin word *pollentia*, the name Romans gave to the general area. Much of Pollença is medieval though there are fine neo-Classical buildings and modern villas.

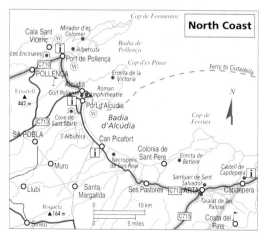

City Sights

Pollença's **Ajuntament** (town hall), north of the central square of Plaça Major, marks the beginning of a flight of 365 stone steps that lead to the **Shrine of Calvary**. Within the chapel is a wooden crucifix, supposedly presented by grateful sailors who survived a shipwreck in the 13th century. On Good Friday a torchlit procession ends here. Also worth seeing are the 15th-century chapel of **Roser Vell**, the church of Sant Jordi and the town's Baroque cathedral, the **Parraguia**.

Pollença is well known for its August fiesta, which commemorates the fighting between Christians and Moors (los *Moros y los Cristianos*), with a mock battle through the town's streets. The other great event is the International Pollença Music Festival, held during July and August in the cloisters of the **Museu de Municipal Pollença**, otherwise known as the Convent of Sant Domenc. Inspired by an Englishman, Philip Newman, in 1962, this festival is one of the great cultural events in Europe and attracts renowned musicians from all over the world. Built in 1578, the Convent of Sant Domenc commemorates the victory of local hero Joan Farragut over the pirate Dragut Rais in 1551. There's a small art museum inside the convent with works from the Middle Ages to the present. Open 11:00–13:00 October–June; 10:00–13:00 and 17:30–20:00 July–September; 10:00–13:00 Sunday; closed Monday.

A must see is Pollenca's Sunday morning market. Fresh fruits, flowers and vegetables are sold in the Plaça Major, while the main car park is developing into a flea market.

Port de Pollença *

Indisputably one of the nicest resorts on the island, Port de Pollença faces one of the best bays in the Mediterranean – best for sheer beauty, for its harbour, watersports and being comparatively unspoilt.

Do not expect loud discos or glitzy nightclubs. Late night entertainment is mostly confined to the hotels – the casual passer-by always welcome – which keeps the streets safe for strolling. The evening *passeig* (stroll) along Port de Pollença's tree-lined promenade is a leisurely ceremony enjoyed by locals, foreign residents and visitors alike. The weekly market is on a Wednesday and, for the determined browser, Port de Pollença offers a fine variety of antique shops, art galleries and boutiques.

Above: *Boats line the harbour at Port de Pollença, one of Mallorca's more relaxed resorts.*
Below: *Breathtaking views from the Mirador d'es Colomer.*

Cala Sant Vicenç, opposite Port de Pollença on the other side of the peninsula, is a long-established artists' colony that has made the transition to up-market resort fairly painlessly. Its comparative remoteness (on Mallorca, nowhere is that far away from anywhere else) has helped prevent holiday apartment blight. Local residents appear to vie with each other over who can produce the most brightly coloured garden.

BIRDWATCHING

The best places for 'twitchers' in Mallorca are the Cases Velles, on the Formentor Peninsula, and the Boquer Valley near Port de Pollença – especially for summer visitors from Africa and the mainland. Flycatchers, chats, redstarts, warblers, ortolans and orioles abound, as do ornithologists, mainly from the UK, Germany, Holland and Scandinavia. Some of the most popular birds are beecatchers, bright balls of colour that swoop and dart in a dazzling display, and nightingales that, far from being rare, can be heard singing throughout the island.

CAP DE FORMENTOR

The Badia de Pollença is made by two finger-like peninsulas, the Cap de Formentor and the Cap d'es Pinar. Cap de Formentor offers secluded, sandy bays and 200m (660ft) high cliffs. A short ferry ride from Port de Pollença is a famous bay called the **Cala Pi de la Posada**, which also boasts the world renowned Formentor Hotel, easily Mallorca's finest. It has been cosseting the great, the good and the merely famous since 1930; casual tourists can enjoy the pine-tree fringed bay without having to check-in.

On the opposite side of the peninsula is one of Mallorca's most famous look-out points, the **Mirador d'es Colomer**, which clings to a mighty, overhanging cliff, giving spectacular sea and coastal views. It can be crowded, as every tourist bus on the island seems to stop there at some time during the day, but is still well worth a visit. If you are lucky enough to be staying in the Pollença area, try to visit this mirador at sunrise or sunset. There is also an old watchtower nearby, the **Albercutx**, which gives views in the opposite direction, over Formentor and Pollença Bay. Cap de Formentor itself has a lighthouse and souvenir shop. The road to it may be unnerving for those unused to driving along steep, narrow tracks, often with sheer drops to the valley below, but you can always walk.

Below: *Cala Pi de la Posada, the pine-fringed white sandy beach of the Formentor Hotel.*

ALCÚDIA

This ancient fortified town began life as a Phoenician settlement, was later held by the Greeks and then established as the capital of Balearis Major by the Roman general Quintus Caecilius Metullus in 123BC. When the Moors took over, they renamed the town *al-Kudia*, meaning literally 'on the hill'. Like many other Mallorcan towns, Alcúdia was built inland from its port to save it from marauding pirates.

Bull-fighting is a major Alcúdian attraction during the summer for Mallorcans who, like the mainland Spanish, do not take kindly to being lectured about cruelty to animals. However if you want to see the spectacle without the gore, trips are arranged here on Thursday evenings to see a mock bullfight at 18:00. The town can become extremely crowded on bull-fighting days and for that reason alone, is best avoided. But otherwise, Alcúdia is one of those magical places, a little reminiscent of Barcelona's famed Gothic Quarter, where the idea is to simply wander around and soak up the atmosphere.

Below: *The small Roman amphitheatre located just outside Alcúdia.*
Opposite: *Part of the impressive medieval walls that still surround Alcúdia.*

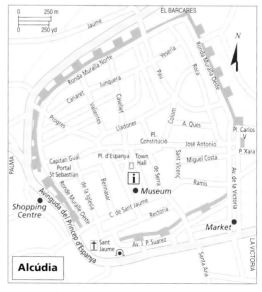

The Old Town

The l5th-century **Xara Gate** is one of two remaining gates in the medieval walls. It leads east to Port d'Alcúdia, while the other gate, known as **Sant Sebastian**, leads west. In between lies Alcúdia's old town, where you can see 16th- and 17th-century houses and the church of **Sant Jaume** which forms the southern bastion in the town walls. The church was founded in the 13th century

and remodelled during the 19th. The **Museu Monográfico de Pollentia** on Carrer de Sant Jaume is a small museum displaying Roman artefacts excavated outside the town walls. Open 10:00–13:30 and 17:00–19:00 April–September; 10:00–13:30 and 15:30–17:30 October–March; closed Saturday and Sunday afternoons and Mondays.

Oratori de Sant Anna *

Just outside the town, on the Port d'Alcúdia road, is the Oratori de Sant Anna, thought to be Mallorca's oldest surviving church, dating from the early 13th century. Its simplicity and tranquility make it well worth a visit.

Roman Remains *

Alcúdia was known as Pollentia in Roman times – meaning power. Traces of Roman villas can be seen just outside the medieval town walls. Better preserved is the **Roman amphitheatre**, 1.5km (1 mile) out of town on the way to the port. The amphitheatre is the smallest in Spain but nevertheless impressive.

MALLORCA'S BEST BEACHES

Badia d'Alcúdia in the northeast is the island's longest beach, spanning 17km (10½ miles) and backed by low-lying, scrub covered dunes in long stretches. **Es Trenc** in the south is long and wide, with white sand and crystal clear water. West of Palma, **Cala Portals Vells** is busier, a series of three smaller beaches shaded by pines. One of the three, El Mago, is a nudist beach. Outside the summer season, the tiny, rocky coves of the north coast are delightful to explore, particularly those at Deià and Valldemossa. Snorkelling is good here, and at **Cala Tuent** on the west coast there's a stony beach near Sa Calobra that rarely gets crowded.

Above: *Smart boats and the local fishing fleet moored in Port d'Alcúdia's harbour.*
Opposite: *Picturesque old windmills dot the interior.*

MALLORCAN APPETIZERS

Mallorca's specialities that many visitors miss include the wonderful range of dried and pickled fruit and vegetables. Fig cakes, sun-dried peppers and tomatoes, pickled capers and sea fennel (*inojo de mar*) are all superb. Local olives, particularly the smaller, green variety, are served as *tapas*, marinated with a variety of wild and cultivated herbs. Gastronomically, the best time to visit is spring or autumn – although genuinely fresh fruit is usually available the whole year round.

Port d'Alcúdia *

This is where the action is: hectic bars and noisy clubs act as a magnet for pleasure-seeking tourists. There's a superb, 9km-long (5 miles) beach as well – actually three sandy beaches that merge into one white strand – and plenty of watersports to indulge in.

Port d'Alcúdia is also a naval base, a ferry terminal for Ciutadella on Menorca and home to a fishing fleet and numerous luxury yachts. You'll find plenty of good (if pricey) fish restaurants, and the town is excellent for souvenir shopping, particularly for straw hats and baskets made from palm leaves.

Aucanada Peninsula ***

Alcúdia's port rests on a sheltered bay at the base of the beautiful Aucanada Peninsula, a rocky headland cloaked in dense pines, jutting out into a turquoise sea. Around the very end, just above the remote **Cap d'es Pinar**, there are walking trails starting from the **Ermita de la Victoria**, a 500-year-old shrine. This is a delightful spot with superb coastal views: leave the car here and walk, or hire a bicycle from Port d'Alcúdia.

SA POBLA

Inland from Port de Alcúdia, on the Central Plain, Sa Pobla sits on land that has been reclaimed from the marshes of S'Albufera. It's an extremely fertile region known as the **Hortas del Poble**, or people's garden, and produces a wide range of vegetables and strawberries, much of which is exported. There's a good Sunday market where you can buy the local fresh produce.

The village itself has been here since 1232 but, because of the presence of a large salt lake nearby, was never considered a particularly healthy or popular place to live. In the early 19th century, however, the lake was drained and the land divided up more democratically into smaller lots. A forest of wind-driven water pumps was introduced and to this day the windmills, although largely disused, remain a trademark of the area.

Sa Pobla is an agricultural town which preserves a lively sense of history. This is particularly evident in mid-January during the feast of St Antoni, when exuberant processions, devil dancers, all-night bonfires and traditional entertainment take place.

Muro *

On the Manacor road from Sa Pobla is the pretty town of Muro, dominated by its monumental **parish church**. Dating from the 13th century but substantially remodelled during the 16th, this is a fine arcaded church with a 46m (153ft) long nave. The town's **bullring** was built from local stone, like many of Muro's other buildings, and stages bullfights during the summer.

There's an interesting **ethnological museum** on Carrer Major, which displays old agricultural implements and Mallorcan crafts in an elegant 17th-century townhouse. It also has an original Moorish patio and waterwheel, and the world's largest collection of *siurells*, tiny pottery whistles in the form of figures painted in red or green on white. Open 10:00–13:00 and 16:00–18:00 October–March; 10:00–14:00 and 17:00–20:00 April–September; 10:00–13:00 Sunday; closed Mondays and holidays.

WINDMILLS

The origin of Mallorca's windmills is a point of debate. Some believe they were introduced in the 7th century, while others say they were not built until 600 years later. Either way, early versions were driven by canvas sails, later replaced by wooden slats. Windmills in Mallorca had two functions: either pumping up water from underground reserves or grinding corn. Several of the windmills still work, wind power having been rediscovered during the fuel crisis of the early 1970s. The biggest concentration, around Sa Pobla, are used to pump water from wells dug by the Moors 1000 years ago, although the mills themselves are a more recent innovation, first introduced in the early 19th century. During the spring, the Sa Pobla plains attract many artists, enchanted by the sails whirring amidst the blossoming almond trees.

SINGING SUPPERS

The Mallorcans have a rather brutal-seeming tendency to eat songbirds and ordering *tordos amb col* from the menu will reveal thrushes wrapped in cabbage leaves. This winged delicacy is trapped in large nets strung out between lines of trees in the island's olive groves. Thrushes fly low, partly to eat the olives and catch the insects which emerge at dusk, partly to avoid being preyed on by larger birds. The season is from late autumn to mid-winter, when the birds have migrated to Mallorca for the warmer climate.

S'Albufera ★★★

Between Sa Pobla and the Badia d'Alcúdia lies the unique wetland reserve of S'Albufera, a conservation area and an important nesting site. S'Albufera was once a lagoon, the name coming from the Arabic *al-Buhayra*, or 'small lake' but its origins are even older: the Roman historian, Pliny, wrote of herons exported from here to Rome (for the table). Later the marshes became a hunting reserve. Once these marshes spread right across the area that is now Sa Pobla, but over the centuries land reclamation and development has restricted S'Albufera to the 800ha (2000 acres) it covers today.

Birds are the main attraction at S'Albufera: over 200 different species have been recorded here. Purple herons, marsh warblers, nightingales, ospreys and falcons are just some of the birds to have been spotted. Footpaths lead over bridges, past hides and around the central lake, Esperança. It is worth visiting for the plant life alone, especially during springtime when delicately coloured wildflowers dot the landscape.

Below: *S'Albufera's marshes are an important nesting site.*

Overall, the park is an oasis of tranquillity and, perhaps for that very reason, is not automatically on every guided tour of the island. If you are a keen birdwatcher, check with the local Tourist Board, who may have details of special tours arranged for true enthusiasts. Try to avoid the heat of the day: morning is usually best, not least because the light is much better for photography. Open 09:00–19:00 daily (17:00 winter).

East From Sa Pobla

By way of complete contrast to S'Albufera, **Can Picafort**, 5km (3 miles) further southeast off the C712, is a thriving package-holiday resort offering family fun, nightlife, and a range of restaurants, souvenir shops and supermarkets. The remains of an ancient necropolis lie just outside the town.

Colònia de Sant Pere ★★

The road now leads to Colònia de Sant Pere and the Ermita de Betlem. This little fishing village is slowly developing into a resort, though at the moment there is still plenty of traditional charm. The village lies at the foot of both the Puig den Ferrutx and the Serra d'Artà, whose dusty surrounding countryside, dotted with almond and olive trees, seems to have barely been touched by the modern world. The beach is good: part rock, part sand.

Ermita de Betlem ★

Sa Colònia de Sant Pere is a good starting point for walks up and around the Ermita de Betlem, some 300m (600ft) high and overlooking Artà to the south. This is a working hermitage, founded in 1805, and the people who live there were attracted by its solitude. The hermits tend to spend most of their time praying, meditating and tending the soil. A short walking trail which starts just behind the Ermita leads to a spectacular panorama of the Badia d'Alcúdia and to the Cap de Formentor beyond.

NON-ALCOHOLIC DRINKS

These include *zumo de naranja* (fresh orange juice) and *zumo de limón* (fresh lemon juice). If you want lots of ice in your drink, ask for *granizado*. The expressions *con gas* and *sin gas* mean fizzy or still. They are applied to all soft drinks and water. Tap water is safe to drink but often tastes salty. Good quality, cheap bottled water is available everywhere. A few bars and cafés might have *horchata*, a milky-white drink made from fresh almonds.

Below: *Sheep graze in the dusty countryside beyond Colònia de Sant Pere.*

Right: *The fortified church of Sant Salvador, Artà.*

Artà *

Originally a Phoenician settlement, Artà's appearance today is that of an atmospheric medieval town dominating the surrounding countryside from its hilltop location. Make your way to the town centre and up the stone stairway that leads to the 19th-century church of **Sant Salvador**. This former Moorish castle is worth seeing for its fortifications – an unusual architectural feature for a church. There are superb views of the town and coast from the battlements. Other places of interest include the **Museu Regional d'Artà** on the Carrer d'Estrella, which displays artefacts excavated from the site of Ses Païsses. Open 10:00–13:00 Monday–Friday.

Ses Païsses ***

An important archaeological site, Ses Païsses lies on the south side of Artà and is a carefully excavated Bronze Age settlement. Founded around 1000BC, Ses Païsses is notable for its perimeter walls, which are almost intact. In the centre is a small hill, from which the foundations and walls of ancient buildings are visible, giving a clear impression of the layout of one of Mallorca's first villages. Open 09:00–13:00 and 14:30–17:00 October–March; 09:00–13:00 and 15:00–19:00 April–September; closed Saturday afternoon and Sunday in winter.

North Coast at a Glance

BEST TIMES TO VISIT

The resorts can be crowded in the high season and, due to the lack of wind, the temperatures can be unbearably hot. **Spring** and early **autumn** are good times to visit.

GETTING THERE

The main route to the area is the C713 from Palma or the C710 from Sóller. There are regular **buses** from Palma and the **airport** to the main resorts.

GETTING AROUND

The best way to see the north coast is by **car**, which you can hire at your resort or at the airport. The main coastal road is the C712. You can get around by **bus**, particularly between the resorts, or **cycle**.

WHERE TO STAY

During the peak summer season accommodation may be difficult to find. Book well in advance, or visit out of season. There are only two campsites on Mallorca – both are in this area and are completely packed in summer.

LUXURY

Formentor, Playa de Formentor, tel: 971 89 91 00, fax: 971 88 51 55. One of the finest hotels on the island, enjoying magnificent gardens and semi-isolation.

Princesa, Avda. Minerva, Port d'Alcúdia, tel: 971 89 29 50, fax: 971 89 27 97 Family hotel, close to seafront.

MID-RANGE

Bahía de Alcúdia, Avda. de la Playa 6, Port d'Alcúdia, tel: 971 54 58 00, fax: 971 54 76 38. A modern hotel situated close to the beach.

Lagomonte, Urb. Lago Menor, Port d'Alcúdia, tel: 971 89 20 00, fax: 971 89 21 73. Good facilities; excellent for families.

Illa d'Or, Colon 265, Port de Pollença, tel: 971 86 51 00, fax: 971 86 42 13. Waterfront hotel with attractive terrace; live entertainment.

Pollença Park, Urb. Uyal, Port de Pollença, tel: 971 86 53 50, fax: 971 86 53 64. Excellent value, good for families.

BUDGET

Hostal Aucanada, c/S'Illot, Aucanada, tel: 971 54 54 02. Reasonably priced basic accommodation.

Luz del Mar, Mendez Nuñez 12, Port de Pollença, tel: 971 53 27 12. Small, charming bed and breakfast.

Camping Platja Blava, between Port d'Alcúdia and Can Picafort, tel: 971 20 38 61. Opposite a sandy beach; swimming pool, tennis courts and restaurant.

Camping Club San Pedro, between Port d'Alcúdia and Artà, tel: 971 23 03 65. Good facilities, tents and chalets for hire in a peaceful setting.

WHERE TO EAT

You'll find plenty of restaurants along the north coast; Port de

Pollença is particularly good.

Becfi, Avda. Anglada Camarasa, Port de Pollença, no telephone. Expensive restaurant favoured by visiting popstars and royalty.

El Pescador, c/de Sant Joan, Colònia de Sant Pere, tel: 971 58 90 78. Excellent: fresh fish a speciality.

La Fortelesa, Carretera Formentor, Port de Pollença, tel: 971 53 10 59. Family restaurant with good home cooking and *tapas*.

Los Faroles, Pg. Saralegui 46, Port de Pollença, no telephone. Simple seafront restaurant with superb basic fish dishes.

Stay, Muelle Nuevo, Port de Pollença, tel: 971 53 00 13. Expensive but excellent international food.

TOURS AND EXCURSIONS

There's plenty to see and do here. Highly recommended are S'Albufera wetlands, Artà for Ses Paisses Talyotic village and the walk from Colònia de Sant Pere to the Ermita de Betlem.

USEFUL CONTACTS

Tourist Offices
Port de Pollença:
Plaça Miquel Capllonch, tel: 971 20 74 70.
Alcúdia: Avda. Juan Carlos I 68, tel: 971 89 26 15, fax: 971 54 65 15.
Can Picafort: Plaça Gabriel Roca 6, tel: 971 85 03 10, fax: 971 52 37 77.
Sail & Surf Pollença, tel: 971 86 53 46.

6
East Coast

Mallorca's east coast is a string of tiny, unspoilt bays hidden between the trees of the Costa dels Pins. Coastal cliffs and undulating hills provide numerous spectacular lookout points and from the lighthouse at **Cap Capdepera** the views can stretch all the way to Menorca on a clear day.

Development in the east is less intensive than in the brash resorts of the south west. Luxury yachts line immaculate marinas and the hillsides behind the Costa dels Pins are sprinkled with white holiday villas. The resorts of **Cala Millor** and **S'Illot** are busy in July and August but relatively tranquil for the rest of the year. The real gem of this coast, however, is the village of **Cala Figuera**, a photographer's dream of pretty fishermen's cottages lining a tranquil inlet, undisturbed by the tourist invasion and coach loads of day-trippers.

Attractions in the east include the three impressive cave systems at **Artà**, **Drac** and **Hams**, all of which are open to the public. There's even a safari park and a park with tropical birds and performing parrots, both worth a visit for those with small children.

A more cerebral experience can be found at the **Ermita de Sant Salvador**, a lovely old monastery on the highest peak of the Serra de Llevant, with stunning views across the whole island and just one of several pleasant walks. Close by is the ruined Castell de Santuari, which on clear days gives a view to the island of Cabrera. The good roads and gentle slopes of this side of the island make ideal cycling country for families.

CLIMATE

The beautiful coastline, protected by the Serra de Llevant, experiences hot and breezy summers (32°C/90°F) and mild winters. Higher in the mountains, the temperatures can be much cooler, although rainfall is not usual.

Opposite: *The smart new marina at the lively resort of Cala d'Or.*

DON'T MISS

*** **Coves del Drac** and **Coves d'Artà:** wonderful underground rock formations.
** **Cala Figuera:** one of Mallorca's prettiest fishing villages, now an upmarket resort.
** **Capdepera:** splendid 14th-century castle.
** **Ermita de Sant Salvador:** spiritual centre with spectacular views.

Below: *The medieval hilltop town of Capdepera, dominated by its 14th-century castle.*

MIRACLE OF THE FOG

On the 18th of December the town's people celebrate La Fiesta de Nostra Senyora d'Esperança. This tells of the Miracle de Sa Boira, or the miracle of the fog. A vast company of Moors attacked Capdepera, then a small village, so that the people had to seek refuge in the castle. Even if they could hold out, they faced death by starvation, so they placed a statue of Our Lady of Hope on the castle battlements. Suddenly a dense fog descended and so terrified the Moors that they fled. The Nostra Senyora de la Esperança chapel was built in the castle in memory of this miracle.

ALONG THE COAST
Cala Ratjada ★

This one-time sleepy fishing village is now a large and lively resort, a favourite with German tourists. It offers all the usual facilities – watersports, lots of restaurants and a hectic nightlife – but is now a little short on local charm. But it's well worth a visit for the **Jardines Casa March**, a private sculpture garden with works by Barbara Hepworth, Auguste Rodin and Henry Moore among the exhibits. Visits must be arranged in advance; contact the local tourist office (tel: 971 56 30 33) for information. There are good beaches nearby at **Cala Guya** and **Cala Molto**. A 2km (1¼ miles) uphill stroll from Cala Ratjada leads to **Capdepera** and its lighthouse: there are terrific coastal views and on a clear day you might be able to see Menorca.

Capdepera ★★

A few kilometres west along the C715 from Cala Ratjada is Capdepera, a medieval town that lies in the shadow of a fine 14th-century castle. Walk around the battlements for far-reaching views along the east coast. Capdepera figures largely in mythology relating to Jaume I's reconquest of Mallorca and the locals hold an annual fiesta on 18 December celebrating the town's deliverance from marauding Moors.

The nearby hills are planted with dwarf palms and Capdepera is Mallorca's basket-making capital. You may be able to watch a demonstration of this traditional handicraft in the town.

Seven kilometres (4½ miles) southeast of Capdepera lies the impressive 14th-century tower of **Torre de Canyamel**. This was originally built as a lookout point from where to watch for pirates.

Coves d'Artà ★★★

The greatest treasure of this stretch of coast lies below, not above, ground. Set into the cliff face above the Platja de Canyamel, the Coves d'Artà are among the most spectacular caves on the island. Some 300m (1000ft) deep, these limestone caves were formed over the centuries by coastal erosion.

Guides lead you through subterranean caverns full of fantastically sculpted stalactites and stalagmites. Inspired by the eerie rock formations, someone – whether an imaginative speleologist or marketing whizz kid – saw fit to name the various chambers after the stages in Dante's *Inferno*. This theme is played up to the hilt, reaching a climax in the deepest cavern, the appositely named 'Inferno', where a tape of Bach's 'horror film' organ music adds to the gothic atmosphere.

East Coast

Left: *Stalagmites contort into fantastic rock formations at the Coves d'Artà.*

In 1230 over a thousand Moors hid here until Jaume I literally smoked them out; the caves have also been an inevitable hideout for pirates. The French author Jules Verne is supposed to have been inspired to write his classic sci-fi novel *Journey to the Centre of the Earth* after visiting the caves. This is an excellent tourist attraction but unfortunately the slippery surfaces of the caves make them unsuitable for the infirm or disabled. Open 09:30–19:00 daily (10:00–17:00 winter).

Further on down the coast the newly developed **Costa dels Pins** is an up-market resort. **Cala Blana** is fairly low-key with man-made beaches, while **Cala Millor** is a fully-fledged package-holiday resort, lined with rather unattractive apartment blocks.

LIMESTONE FORMATIONS

The bizarre rock formations in Mallorca's cave systems have formed over millions of years. Stalactites are formed as groundwater seeps through porous limestone to the roof of a cave, picking up traces of calcium bicarbonate in the process. Water and carbon dioxide evaporate from the droplets clinging to the cave ceiling, leaving a tiny deposit of calcium carbonate. Over time, the deposits build up to create icicle-like shapes, the streaks of colour coming from impurities in the minerals. Stalagmites, the formations that rise from the cave floor, are created in a similar way.

Reserva Africana *

At the southern end of the Badia d'Artà is Mallorca's own safari park covering a 40ha (100 acres) site. This is excellent value for a family outing. Animals include lions, zebras, antelope and ostriches, plus the inevitable monkeys who are as cheeky here as in any other safari park. You can use your own car, or travel on one of the safari trucks. Afterwards, there is a Baby Zoo to visit featuring young animals that have been born there. Open 09:00–19:00 daily (09:00–17:00 winter). A free bus service runs from Cala Bona, Cala Millor and Sa Coma.

S'Illot *

Close by is the tiny fishing village of S'Illot. This rarely appears in tourist brochures, and the Mallorcans themselves are extremely fond of it. S'Illot is as close as you can get to old Mallorca on the east coast but, as the developers move in, it is changing fast and turning into the standard cluster of villas and hotels.

Talayotic Remains *

In S'Illot, follow signs to the remains of an ancient talayotic settlement (*see* p.10), thought to have been inhabited in 1300BC. At first glance, the village looks like a pile of stones but with a map it is possible to distinguish the boundary wall with its gateway, the sanctuary and the main monument, or place of worship, under which there is a subterranean lake. A second settlement at nearby **Cala Morlanda** has not yet been excavated.

Porto Cristo *

Following the C717 brings you to Porto Cristo, a little way down the east coast from **Sa Coma**. A bustling holiday resort, Porto Cristo retains plenty of its original atmosphere as a fishing port. In 1936, 12,000 men from the neighbouring island Menorca took the port for the Republican cause. The occupation lasted just a few weeks, everyone either drifting home or being captured, but it was the only serious action the Balearics saw during the Civil War. Porto Cristo's main attraction is an **aquarium** on the Carrer de Vella stocked with exotic fish from around the world, including piranhas and electric eels. Open 09:00–19:00 daily.

> ### COVES
>
> Coves, or *calas*, are a good alternative to the traditional sandy beach. Although predominantly rock (you might want to bring something soft to lie on), there are often small areas of sand to be found. The water is deep and ideal for diving or swimming. It's a welcome contrast to the larger bays where the gently shelving sand is ideal for small children, but can be frustrating for the serious swimmer.

Opposite: *Ostriches are just some of the exotic creatures who live at the Reserva Africana.*
Below: *The popular resort of Porto Cristo with its lovely sandy beach.*

Coves del Drac ★★★

Much of the success of Porto Cristo among tourists is its proximity to the amazing natural phenomenon of the Coves del Drac (dragon caves). The caves are estimated to contain some 2km (1½ miles) of tunnels and caverns. In the centre is the 177m long (580ft) Llac Martel (Lake Martel, named after the French speleologist Edouard-Alfred Martel, who first explored them). Concerts are held several times a day on the lake, the musicians floating in boats as the whole ensemble is illuminated by torches. Caverns called by fanciful names like Diana's Baths and the Theatre of the Fairies glow with their natural colours enhanced by discreetly placed spotlights. Open 10:00–17:00 daily (winter 10:30–16:00).

Above: *An invitation, in Castilian, to the eerie 'dragon caves'.*
Opposite: *A row of charming houses bathed in Mediterranean light line Porto Colom's harbour.*

Coves dels Hams ★★

The Caves of Hams, called after the Mallorcan word for fish-hooks which many of the stalactites are supposed to resemble, are 3km (2 miles) northwest of Porto Cristo on the road to Manacor. Although smaller than Drac or Artà, they are nonetheless impressive. There are seven main caverns and an underground lake called the Sea of Venice, all enhanced by a sound and light show. What sets these caves apart from Artà and Drac is the near-translucent whiteness of their stalactites and stalagmites, caused by high calcium carbonate levels in the limestone. Open 10:30–13:20; 14:45–16:30 daily, summer only.

Further along, towards Porto Colom, and just inland from Cala Falco, are the **Coves del Pirata**, or Pirate's Caves. Nowhere near as spectacular as those at Artà, Drac or Hams and less likely to have been used by pirates than any of the others, they nonetheless can afford an hour or so's pleasure.

TOP TIPS FOR KIDS

Mallorca is an ideal family destination with plenty for children to do:

- Admire the underground scenery at the caves of Drac, Hams or Artà.
- Watch performing parrots at the Exotic Parque los Pajaros, Cales de Mallorca.
- Whizz down the water-slides at Hidropark or Aquapark in Magaluf.
- See dolphins and seals at Marineland, Costa d'en Blanes.
- Spot the lions at the Reserva Africana.
- Ride the wooden tram from Palma to Sóller.
- Check out the cacti at Botanicactus, Ses Salines.

Exotic Parque Los Pajaros *

One of Mallorca's more unusual attractions lies on the road between the Cales de Mallorca and Porto Colom. The Exotic Parque los Pajaros (Parrot Park) features tropical birds, a cactus garden and performing parrots, which children will love. Open 10:00–19:00 daily.

Porto Colom **

Set on a natural inlet, Porto Colom is yet another Mediterranean village that claims to have been the birthplace of Christopher Columbus. As it is, Porto Colom is now the centre of all the neighbouring seaside resorts, largely because it used to be the port for the large inland town Felanitx. Some parts of the old town remain to wander around. The fish restaurants on its wide front have a deservedly good reputation. There are a few shops, a diving school that offers trips out to sea in a glass-bottomed boat and a mini-train that links Porto Colom with **Cala d'Or**, a busy resort to the south and an intriguing mixture of the brash and the relaxed.

The area centres around a small lagoon and a pleasant, white-walled holiday complex dating from 1932. Beyond that things become a little more noisy and extremely crowded; beaches like **Cala Gran** or **Cala Longa** are often near to insufferable in the high season. Cala d'Or also shares a marina with Porto Colom and offers very good all-round sporting facilities.

CHRISTOPHER COLUMBUS

Numerous villages and towns in Spain claim links with Columbus. Locals in Porto Colom believe the explorer was born in their village, although this is not a proven fact; he may only have sailed from here on one expedition.

More confusion arises from the fact that Columbus never actually set foot on mainland USA. He sailed west from Spain in 1492, hoping to find a new route to Asia and landed on a small island in the Bahamas. Over the next five years he went on to discover Cuba, Jamaica, Venezuela, Panama, Puerto Rico and what is now Haiti and the Dominican Republic.

Even the location of his remains is questionable. In 1899, many years after his death, when Cuba ceased to be a Spanish colony, what were thought to be the bones of Columbus were brought to Sevilla on the mainland. No-one really knows, however, whether the right remains were brought across.

HERMITS

Monks or hermits, distin-
guished by their simple
woollen robes and flowing
beards, live in the tiny *ermitas*
and *santuaris* of Mallorca. To
become a hermit, a novice
must spend a trial period at the
Ermita de Betlem, near Artà.
The lifestyle is a modest one;
hermits follow a strict schedule
of rising to pray at 1am and
then again at dawn, spending
the daylight hours praying,
meditating and working the
soil before retiring to their
simple cells at 9pm.
    Some of the tiny
monasteries accept guests,
providing basic accommodation and meals, usually in a
beautiful, tranquil setting. Try
the **Ermita del Puig de Maria**
at Pollença, the **Monasteri
Cura de Randa** and the larger
Monasteri de Lluc.

Below: *A stone cross on
the road that ascends to
Ermita de Sant Salvador.*

Ermita de Sant Salvador

A worthwhile excursion a few kilometres inland from
Porto Colom, however, is one Mallorca's most famous
spiritual attractions, the Ermita de Sant Salvador. At
509m (1600ft) it is the highest point of the Serra de
Llevant, visible from miles around because of its massive
stone outcrops. It is reached by a small road that twists
and turns its way to the small plateau on which stands
the 13th-century monastery. Once parked, you can drink
from the centuries-old well and breathe in the clear,
fresh air while enjoying panoramic views over the
island. There's a lovely Gothic panel of the Last Supper
in the gatehouse. The simplest of accommodation,
always spotless, is available for overnight stays.

Three kilometres (2 miles) south of the Ermita lies the
ruined **Castell de Santuari**. The castle was built by
Jaume II on the site of a Moorish fortress. There are
fantastic views from the ramparts, and on a good day
you can see clear to the island of Cabrera, some 40km (25
miles) away. Open 10:00–19:00 daily.

Cala Figuera **

This is one of the prettiest resorts on the east coast. Cala
Figuera is still a fishing village, set on a steep-sided inlet,
and when they are not out at sea, the town's fishermen
can be found at the
harbour mending their
nets. It is one of the
most picturesque places
imaginable and even
manages to survive the
coachloads of tourists
seeking the ultimate,
Mallorcan destination. A
daily influx of visitors
cram into the few bars
and fish restaurants in
the high season and then
leave the town much as
it was before.

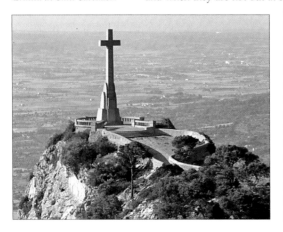

East Coast at a Glance

The climate is reasonable all year round but the resorts get busy in peak season and accommodation will be difficult to find then. **Spring** and late **summer** are the best times to go; winters are mild.

To get to the east coast, take the C715 **road** which runs inland from Palma to Cala Ratjada. **Buses** run from Palma and the **airport** to the resorts.

There is no major coastal **road** linking the resorts; you'll have to take a succession of minor roads. **Car** is by far the best way of travelling around.

Accommodation is very hard to find during the summer. The resorts, Cala Ratjada in particular, tend to be block-booked by tour operators.

LUXURY

Cala d'Or, Avda. Bélgica s/n, Cala d'Or, tel: 971 65 72 49, fax: 971 65 93 51. Elegant hotel in picturesque setting; swimming pool, terraces, restaurant and beach bar.
Hotel el Vistamar, Hermanas Pinzón Porto Colom, tel: 971 82 51 01, fax: 971 82 50 05. Refurbished four star with pool and large garden.
Lillot, c/Hernán Cortés 41, Cala Ratjada, tel: 971 81 82 84. Very smart, central hotel.

MID-RANGE

Cala Marsal, Platja Cala Marsal, Porto Colom, tel: 971 82 52 25, fax: 971 82 52 50. Large family hotel; swimming pool, tennis court.
Las Palomas, Asunción 14, Porto Colom, tel: 971 82 52 52, fax: 971 82 49 61. Medium-sized 3-star hotel; swimming pool, squash courts.
Ses Rotjes, Rafael Blanes 21, Cala Ratjada, tel: 971 56 43 45, fax: 971 56 31 08. Small, attractive hotel with excellent Michelin star-rated restaurant. Not suitable for children.
Talayot, Son Sard, tel: 971 58 53 14, Cala Millor, fax: 971 58 50 66. Central, friendly hotel with swimming pool.

BUDGET

Jaume, Mestre Vicenç Nadal 65, Cala Ratjada, tel: 971 56 30 80. Small, central hotel with swimming pool.
Corona, Pg. Colón, Cala Rajada, tel: 971 56 38 04. Two-star central hotel with picturesque views.

Fish restaurants abound in the resorts; many places also specialize in Mallorcan cooking.
Celler Can Faro, Mestral 4, Artà, tel: 971 56 21 03. Busy, pleasant restaurant serving good Mallorcan food.
Bistro, c/Andres Roig 7, Cala d'Or, tel: 971 65 81 10. Expensive; with an excellent charcoal grill.
Yate d'Or, Avda. Belgica 4, Cala d'Or, tel: 971 65 79 78. Specialises in seafood. Ask for a table on the patio.
Can Martina, Pg. des Port, Porto Petro, tel: 971 65 75 17. Picturesque fish restaurant; try the seafood paella.
Can Pep Noguera, Ctra Pto Colom–Pto Cristo, tel: 971 57 33 55. Good country food; specialities are guinea fowl and snails.
S'Era de Pula, c/de Son Servera–Capdepera, tel: 971 56 79 40. Expensive, classic Mallorcan food in an old farmhouse.

Tours to the Caves at Drac and Hams are arranged from most resorts, as are tours to the Safari Park and the Parrot Park. One of the best excursions is a 4km (2½-mile) walk from the Castell de Santuari via the Puig de sa Comuna to the Ermita de Sant Salvador. The route, marked by yellow and red paint splashes on rocks and trees, begins in a valley orchard and climbs gently through a sea of wild flowers and herbs. Allow up to 2 hours for the ascent, half an hour less for the descent.

Tourist Offices
Cala Ratjada: Plaça dels Pins, tel: 971 56 30 33.
Cala Millor: c/de Fetjet 4, tel: 97158 58 64.
Porto Cristo: c/de Gual 31, tel: 971 82 09 31.

7
South Coast

Mallorca's south coast was until recently one of the most remote and unknown parts of the island, from the sweeping sand dunes of **Es Trenc** to the salt flats of **Salines de Llevant**. The coast and its hinterland offers a series of extremes interspersed with moments of pure magic, like the turquoise cove at **Cala Pi** or the important Bronze Age settlement at **Capocorb Vell**. It is a place of quiet woods and wildflowers on the road to the resort of Colònia Sant Jordi, of tall cacti in the strange tourist attraction of **Botanicactus**, and of a still lingering melancholy on the island of **Cabrera** where so many French prisoners died during the Napoleonic War. This area also has Mallorca's only spa; the hot springs at **Banyos de Sant Joan** were equally well known to the Romans for their curative properties and today there is a small hotel offering treatments.

The far south remains relatively undeveloped, with just a handful of resorts. **Colònia de Sant Jordi** is located on a rocky headland next to the sweep of Es Trenc, while at the other end of the beach, S'Estanyol and Sa Rapita have merged into a blur of holiday apartments. Around the Cap Blanc headland, beyond the exquisite coastal scenery of Cala Pi, the scenery is made up of scrubland and steep cliffs. From the beginning of the **Platja de Palma**, however, there's almost continuous development starting with the big resort of **S'Arenal**, following a trail of neon lights, bars, amusement parks and hotels and ending just outside Palma at Can Pastilla.

MENORCA

Ciutadella

Santa Margalida

Arta

PALMA DE MALLORCA

Porto Cristo

MALLORCA

CLIMATE

The south coast has a lovely sea breeze to cool the summer heat. With summer temperatures of 32°C (90°F), the magnificent blue skies are rarely tainted with clouds. During the winter the temperatures call fall below 10°C (50°F) and there may be outbreaks of rain.

Opposite: *Botanicactus is an oasis of leafy calm in southern Mallorca.*

DON'T MISS

*** **Platja d'es Trenc:** a wilderness by the sea.
*** **Cabrera:** a remote island populated only by seabirds.
*** **Capocorb Vell:** remarkable Bronze Age remains.
** **Cala Pi:** beautiful unspoilt coastal scenery.
** **S'Arenal:** for sheer excitement and vitality.

SANTANYI

A few kilometres inland from the coast, **Santanyí** is famous for providing the sandstone used so extensively in Mallorcan architecture. It was once a walled town, as you can see from the Porta Murada, now in the Plaça Port, and is dominated by the church of Sant Andreu.

Campos *

From Santanyí, follow the C717 to the quiet agricultural town of Campos. It has interesting 16th-century buildings, notably the renovated town hall with a coat-of-arms on its façade and a double horseshoe-vaulted entrance; and an impressive church which contains a painting thought to be by Murillo. Campos has a reputation for making excellent cakes and pastries.

Banyos de Sant Joan *

Take the northwest road from Ses Salines to Banyos de Sant Joan, a couple of kilometres further on the way to Campos. Visitors have been taking the waters at these hot springs since Roman times and the current spa has been renovated in traditional Mallorcan style.

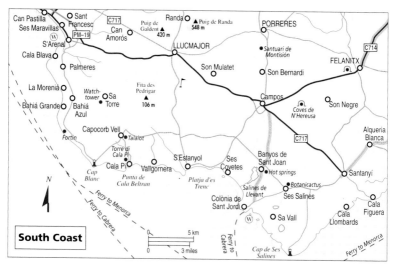

SES SALINES AND THE SALINES DE LLEVANT

A few kilometres to the west of Santanyí is Ses Salines, a village that lies at the heart of Mallorca's salt industry. To the south stretch several kilometres of remote, huge salt flats, where salt is extracted from seawater by the age old evaporation method. It was Mallorca's original salt trade that made it such a prize in ancient times.

Saltpans provide ideal feeding grounds for wading birds such as the black-winged stilt. Drive down to **Cap de Ses Salines** and observe the remarkable plants and birdlife. Much of the land around this southernmost tip is owned by the wealthy March banking family, which means that visitors can no longer stray off the beaten track or roam around the saltpans without prior permission.

Botanicactus **

Close to Ses Salines lies Botanicactus, a 15ha (37 acres) botanical garden with a remarkable collection of over 12,000 cacti, some of which flower exotically and others of a kind you find in cowboy movies. Another section of the park displays wetland plants and a typical Mallorcan garden. Open 09:00–19:00 daily.

Colònia de Sant Jordi*

This busy little port – the port of Campos, 12km (7½ miles) north – on the west side of Cap de Ses Salines is reputed to have been a haven for smugglers during Franco's dictatorship. Today it's a growing resort, with numerous bars and restaurants for visitors to choose from. From here you can take a boat trip around the coast or to the island of Cabrera.

> ### SALT
>
> Ses Salines takes its name from being a source of salt, which was first extracted by the Romans. The area was ideal for large-scale salt production – winter storms roll over the flat beaches to deposit frothy water on the *cocons*, or salt pans, which are then dried out by the hot summer sun, leaving a hard crystalline layer.
>
> The extraction process has not changed and the salt pans can be visited today, along with the lakes of S'Estany de ses Gambes and Es Tamarells, both important nesting grounds for migratory birds. Spring is the best time to visit.

Below: *Mallorca's southern beaches are far less crowded than elsewhere on the island.*

CALA PI WALK

An old fishermen's trail runs along the clifftop from Cala Pi west to the watchtower at Sa Torre. The walk takes about two hours in each direction and on a windy day is an exhilarating stroll. The scenery is full of contrasts: magnificent views across the blue sea to Cabrera are offset against dramatic red sandstone and limestone cliffs and rock formations, while wild herbs scent the air and seagulls shriek overhead. The views back to the bottle-green pines and deep turquoise water of Cala Pi make it worth even the first 20 minutes, for a gentler stroll.

CABRERA

Eighteen kilometres (11 miles) off the south coast, Cabrera is a wild and craggy island that has been a protected National Park since 1991. Visits are restricted to ornithologists, scientists and day trippers. Wild goats, unusual lizards and rare birds all thrive in this unspoilt habitat. Measuring a scant 7km by 5km (4½ by 3 miles) and with the tiniest of permanent human populations, Cabrera is a peaceful and, for nature lovers, absorbing place to spend the day. Take your swimming things and a snorkel and fins if you have them, for the Cabrera waters are wonderfully clear.

Platja d'es Trenc ★★★

This wide bay to the west of Colònia de Sant Jordi has long been recognised as one of Mallorca's most perfect, unspoilt beaches, popular with nudists. Imagine a beach surrounded by pines, only reluctantly giving way to the low, rolling dunes that guard 7km (4½ miles) of pure white sand and turquoise sea. The whole area is actually protected by law – although for how much longer Mallorca's rapacious developers will be kept at bay remains to be seen. Generally the water is remarkably clear. **Ses Covetes** is a small village at the western end of Platja d'es Trenc where you can find several simple bars and casual restaurants, after having driven down the original long and winding (and dusty) road, past old stone farmhouses and picturesque windmills.

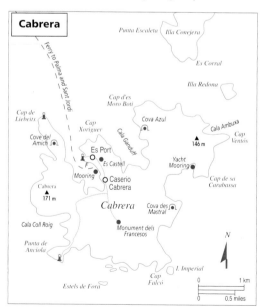

Cala Pi *

A short drive west of Platja d'es Trenc is what used to be Mallorca's most closely guarded secret, the beach of Cala Pi. Luxury villas and apartment buildings are being built around this tiny rocky cove and there are plans to build a marina. Go and see Cala Pi while there is still time and climb down the steep stone steps to sunbathe on the most perfect of little beaches.

Capocorb Vell ***

Some 5km (3 miles) inland from Cala Pi are the Bronze Age remains at Capocorb Vell, dating from 1000BC. The ancient buildings are well preserved, with some roofs and doorways still in place, so that you can begin to imagine how the people lived. There are five *talayots* near the main group of buildings, scattered over the surrounding fields. The philanthropist Archduke Ludwig Salvador (*see* p. 55) put up the money to excavate the site and the 28 Bronze Age buildings are considered to be one of Spain's most important national monuments. Open 10:00–17:00 Friday–Wednesday.

Above: *Luxury apartments line the headland at Cala Pi.*

PLATJA DE PALMA

Cala Pi is essentially the last resort on this southern coastline, which curves round in a series of rocky headlands dotted with small villages to the Platja de Palma, a long, straight, highly developed beachfront leading from S'Arenal in the south to Can Pastilla, virtually at the end of the runway of the island's main airport, southeast of Palma.

This is the place to come for superb beaches, high rise buildings, neon-lit nights and the pounding disco beat. From S'Arenal to Palma there's one souvenir shop after another, enlivened by the occasional amusement arcade. The clientele tends to be either German or English and the well developed infrastructure makes the area very attractive to families.

MARINE LIFE

Mallorca's rocky shores mean the water is astonishingly clear and the snorkelling is good, particularly around Cabrera, where the lack of development has left the marine life undisturbed. Common species include sea urchins, mussels, clams, cuttlefish, sea anenomes, crabs, prawns, jellyfish and squid, as well as several species of fish native to the waters of the Balearics. For divers, there are several interesting wrecks to explore. Equipment can be hired from several centres around the coast of Mallorca.

Below: *S'Arenal's Aquacity is an enormous fun-filled waterpark.*

S'Arenal ★★

This resort has been unashamedly designed for people who like fun in the sun. S'Arenal is well run and offers a huge range of attractions including a large waterpark, **Aquacity**, which is great for families. The beaches are close to being standing room only, but no-one seems to mind. It is all extremely good natured and children in particular seem to adore it.

A train runs along the 7km (4½ miles) seafront between S'Arenal and Can Pastilla on the outskirts of Palma but if you can, try walking it at night, just for the experience of seeing so many bars, discos, souvenir shops and dubious night clubs all jostling for your attention. And if you're hankering for a pint of bitter or a plate of fish and chips, you won't leave S'Arenal disappointed.

Just outside S'Arenal lies **Aquacity**, which again is well worth a visit. It is legitimately billed as the world's largest, and best water funfair. Choose from swimming pools designed to look like country lakes, water slides that are akin to your first free-fall parachute jump, or a wave pool which really does produce huge waves. There is also a parrot show, a model farm, a small zoo and, with a delightful touch of sheer eccentricity, a collection of antique typewriters. Open 10:00–17:00, May–October.

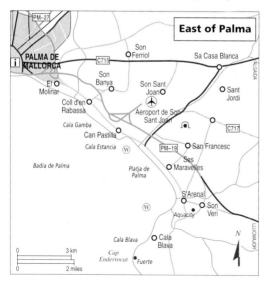

South Coast at a Glance

BEST TIME TO VISIT

With cooling sea breezes, the south coast is very pleasant during the summer. **Springtime** is the season to watch the migrating birds. It can be rainy during the winter and temperatures may fall below 10°C (50°F).

GETTING THERE

The C717 runs from Palma to Santanyi; the PM-1 (motorway) from Palma to S'Arenal. The **bus** service is good along these routes but not so frequent along the minor **roads** leading to the coast.

GETTING AROUND

Apart from the coastal **road** linking S'Arenal with Can Pastilla, there are only a succession of minor roads along the coast. If you wish to explore the coast the best way to do it is by **car**.

WHERE TO STAY

Accommodation is cheaper along the south coast – even the high-rise hotels in S'Arenal and Can Pastilla cost less than those on the 'Maganova coast', southwest of Palma.

LUXURY

Tres Playas, Cala Esmeralda, Colònia de Sant Jordi–Ses Salines, tel: 971 65 51 51, fax: 971 65 56 44. High-class modern hotel with good sea views. Indoor and outdoor pools, tennis court.
El Cid, Ctra. S' Arenal km8,

Can Pastilla, tel: 971 26 08 50, fax: 971 85 14 24. Medium-sized 3-star family hotel with a range of sports; facilities for the disabled.
Sur Mallorca, Pça Cristóbal Colón, Colònia de Sant Jordi, tel: 971 65 52 00. Large, friendly, family hotel close to the beach.

MID-RANGE

Balneario de Sant Joan de Font Santa, Ctra. Campos, tel: 971 65 60 16, fax: 971 65 50 16. Peaceful retreat set in large garden, patronized mainly by visitors to the thermal springs.
Calma, Horacio 5, Can Pastilla, tel: 971 26 11 50. Friendly, relaxed hotel close to beach.
Playa d'Or, Virgilio 26, Can Pastilla, tel: 971 26 01 62. Quiet hotel with swimming pool, overlooking beach.
Romántica, Carabela 4, Colònia de Sant Jordi, tel: 971 65 53 25, fax: 971 65 53 50. Large, central hotel with disco, indoor and outdoor pools.

BUDGET

Albergue Platja de Palma, c/Costa Brava 17, Can Pastilla, tel: 971 26 08 92. Clean, basic youth hostel, very close to the seafront.
Hotel Casa Chiquita, Esmeralda 14, Colonia Sant Jordi, tel: 971 65 51 21, fax: 971 65 54 13. Small, modern hostel with garden, 150m from beach.
Colonial, Gabriel Roca 9, Colònia de Sant Jordi, tel: 971

64 52 78. Small family run hotel in the port area.
Es Turo, Ingeniero Roca 38, Colònia de Sant Jordi, tel: 971 65 50 57. Small, central hotel with good view of the beach; bar and terrace.

WHERE TO EAT

Plenty of choice for burgers along the Platja de Palma, but traditional Mallorcan food is more difficult to find. However there are good fish restaurants.
El Puerto, c/de Port 13, Colònia de Sant Jordi, tel: 971 65 60 47. Excellent fresh fish and tasty paella.
El Rancho Picadero, c/de Flamenco 1, Can Pastilla, tel: 971 26 10 02. Ranch-style restaurant with barbeque and roast meat.
Ses Roques, c/de Colònia de Sant Jordi, tel: 971 65 10 47. Mallorcan dishes and seafood.
S'Escar, Ses Covettes, at the western end of the Platja d'es Trenc, tel: 971 83 82 73. Beach bar/restaurant with good fresh fish.

TOURS AND EXCURSIONS

The top tour is the day-long trip to Cabrera. Within easy distance are the Manacor pearl factories and the wine cellars at Binissalem. A special bus runs along the coast from Magaluf to Aquacity.

USEFUL CONTACTS

Tourist Office: c/Dr Barraquer 5, Colònia de Sant Jordi, tel: 971 65 54 37.

8
Central Plain

If anywhere can be said to embody the old Mallorca it is the Central Plain (Es Pla) – now, alas, semi-deserted during the day as many inhabitants have better paying jobs in the resort towns on the coast. Nonetheless it is still an extremely attractive area: in spring the almond blossoms resemble a snow-white sea. Because it is so flat, it is ideally suited for cycling, which allows you to explore many hidden and half-forgotten corners.

There is actually quite a lot to explore on the Central Plain. The town of **Inca** is the heart of the island's leather industry and is crammed with visitors in search of bargains during the day. **Casa Serra**, an old house near the town of Petra, is the birthplace of Junípero Serra, the Franciscan friar who in the 18th century established missions at what are now the principal cities of the USA's west coast. **Manacor** is the place to shop for high quality artificial pearls and at the **Puig de Randa** there are three monasteries, the main one founded by the Mallorcan philosopher Ramón Llull.

The easiest way to tour Es Pla is by hire car or bicycle, taking separate excursions along the three main arterial routes from Palma. Minor roads criss-cross between the villages and while a few hills jut out of the plain, the landscape has none of the west coast's hair-raising curves.

Entertaining excursions include wine-tasting at **Binissalem** or watching the age-old skill of glass-blowing at **Casa Gordiola**. Children and fans of the bizarre will have fun at the **Son Gual Parc Prehistòric**, where enormous plastic dinosaurs loom out of the bush.

MENORCA
Ciutadella
Inca
PALMA DE MALLORCA Felanitx
MALLORCA

CLIMATE

Sheltered by the mountains to the west, the central plain is a rich argicultural zone, with strong sunshine to ripen olives, apricots and figs. The fierce summer sun can be unrelenting at 34°C (93°F). Watch out for chilly nights, especially in the winter and spring, when a hot day can turn very cool by nightfall.

Opposite: *Central Mallorca is peppered with picturesque windmills which have formed part of the landscape for hundreds of years.*

DON'T MISS

*** Manacor: impressive artificial pearl industry.
*** Casa Serra: birthplace of the founder of the Californian missions.
*** Puig de Randa: for three monasteries and views of the whole island.
** Inca: for high quality leather goods.
** Binissalem: taste Mallorca's local wines.
* Algaida: glassblowing, prehistoric monsters and devil dancing if you're lucky.

FROM PALMA TO INCA AND SINEU

Santa Maria del Camí *

Fourteen kilometres (9 miles) northeast of Palma is Santa Maria del Camí, an old market town with some interesting buildings. Don't miss the parish church, which has a lovely 18th-century belltower decorated with blue tiles. The enormous Baroque former Convent dels Minims now houses a *bodega* (wine shop) where you can taste local wines. Local nuns also produce cakes and biscuits for which the town is well known – buy them direct from the Convent de las Jerónimas.

Binissalem **

This is the headquarters of Mallorca's wine-making industry. Vines were introduced by the Romans, although only a few hundred acres are under cultivation today. Binissalem is one of Spain's newest DO's

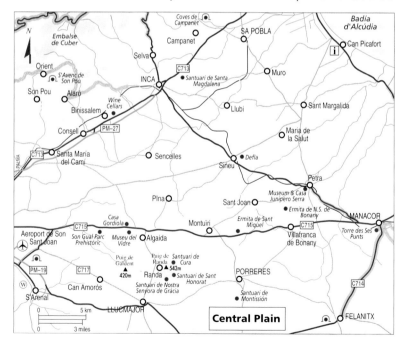

Central Plain

(*Denominación de Origen* – which guarantees a reasonable quality) and produces mainly red wines. The best are made from the local *manto negro* grape; local producers whose wines are worth seeking out and tasting are José Ferrer, Franja Roja and Herederos.

A week-long wine festival is held after the grape harvest (end of September or early October) and there's plenty of dancing, fireworks and wine-tasting to be enjoyed.

Inca **

The third largest town on the island, Inca dominates the local leather trade and, while prices are no cheaper than anywhere else, the choice is far greater. Organised tours converge on the Thursday morning market, most taking in a leather factory visit as well. The town is not particularly picturesque but it's well worth stopping off to sample traditional Mallorcan cuisine in one of the old wine-cellar restaurants. On the second Thursday in November there's *Díjous Bo* – the biggest agricultural fair on the island, with street markets and folk dancing.

Just east of Inca is the small **Santuari de Santa Magdalena** perched on top of a 304m (1113ft) high peak, from where there are extensive views of the surrounding countryside.

Sineu **

Thirty kilometres (20 miles) from Palma, and to the southeast of Inca, Sineu stands virtually at the centre of the island. Jaume II built a palace here in the 13th century, which remained a favourite royal residence until the 16th century, when it became a convent. Today the nuns here are still known as the *monges del palau* (palace nuns).

There's a lively weekly market on Wednesdays that specializes in livestock. Thousands of animals are bought and sold but unless you're a farmer it's probably not a major tourist attraction.

Below: *The flat Central Plain is ideal for exploring by bicycle.*

Above: *Painted tiles decorate the shrine to Mallorcan philisopher Ramón Llull at the Santuari de Sant Honorato.*

FROM PALMA TO LLUCMAJOR AND RANDA

Llucmajor *

Mallorca's independence came to an abrupt end here in 1349 when Jaume III was defeated in battle by his cousin Pedro IV of Aragón. The old battlefield of Llucmajor, 25km (15 miles) southeast of Palma, is now an important agricultural town with good markets on Wednesday and Sunday. It stands on a plateau overlooking fields lined with old windmills.

Puig de Randa ***

Head north towards Algaida for 4km (2½ miles), until you arrive at the turn off for **Randa**. This is a delightful village lying below the 548m (1709ft) tall Puig de Randa that looms out of the flat lands of the Central Plain and is the starting point for a unique pilgrimage to three old monasteries – well worth the effort.

Signs along the way lead you to each of the three sanctuaries along the winding mountain road. First is the medieval **Santuari Nostra Senyora de Gràcia** where there are superb views of the south coast. Higher still stands the **Santuari de Sant Honorato**. The **Santuari de Cura** crowns the peak of the Puig de Randa. The Mallorcan philosopher Ramón Llull founded this monastery in the 13th century after the end of his scandalous love affair with a married woman, spending most of his time in solitary contemplation. Superb stained glass windows in the church detail the life and works of this extraordinary man. It's possible to spend the night in one of the small, spare but scrupulously clean cells.

Montuïri *

Northeast of Randa, high on a ridge surrounded by old stone windmills, stands the small town of Montuïri. Aside from the windmills and the 13th-century church, Montuïri's biggest attractions are the excellent Monday market and the **Ermita de Sant Miquel**, a 19th-century chapel some 2km (1¼ miles) to the east.

Algaida *

North of Randa is Algaida, a peaceful market town that explodes into life during the feast of Sant Jaume (24–26 July) when devil dancers perform in one of the island's oldest celebrations. These colourful characters were once banned by the church but now form an intrinsic part of many fiestas, throwing firecrackers into the crowds and generally indulging in anarchic behaviour.

Casa Gordiola*

Off the C715, 2km (1¼ miles) northwest from Algaida, heading back towards Palma, is a mock-medieval castle called the Casa Gordiola that actually only dates back to 1969. On the other hand, the Gordiola family that built it has been making superb glass since 1719. There's an interesting museum here and a workshop, where visitors can watch craftsmen create the most delicate or utilitarian handblown objects, most of which can be bought from the showrooms. Open 09:00–20:00 Monday–Saturday (19:00 winter); 09:00-13:00 Sunday.

Children will love the **Son Gual Parc Prehistòric**, a prehistoric theme park off the C715 road from Casa Gordiala to Palma. Life-sized plastic dinosaurs lurk in the bush. Open 10:00–20:00 daily.

> **RAT IN THE KITCHEN**
>
> Field rats abound in the Central Plain and are, on special occasions, served up as a delicacy. The recipe calls for extensive cleaning and at least three different types of cooking – marinating, boiling and then roasting or grilling. The taste is said to be similar to rabbit.

Below: *Glass-blowers at Casa Gordiola practise their traditional craft.*

FROM PALMA TO MANACOR
Manacor ★★★

Some 47km (29 miles) due east of Palma, Mallorca's
second largest town, Manacor, was founded by Jaume II
in the 13th century. It's a fairly industrialized town, and
Manacor is unique inasmuch as there are no significant
archaeological remains to be seen. It is also the home of
Mallorca's artificial pearl industry and you can visit
some of the factories to watch glass beads being coated
with an iridescent glaze, the ingredients of which are
theoretically a secret. Pottery and cabinet making are the
other two main industries and the souvenir shops are
packed with ceramics and wooden carvings.

Església del Dolors ★

Worth seeking out is Manacor's parish church, the
Església del Dolors, or Church of the Sorrows, built on
the site of a mosque – which possibly explains the
famous, minaret-like clocktower. This church is part of
the convent of Sant Domenc which also has a beautiful
17th-century cloister. Near the church is a medieval
tower called the **Torre de Ses Punts**, noted for its
unusual Gothic windows and, less so, for a collection of
ancient coins found locally. Manacor also has a horse-
trotting track but the main attraction for visitors still
seems to be the opportunity to watch both artificial
pearls and pottery being made. Parking can be difficult,
so leave your car on the outskirts of town and walk.

Petra

Ten kilometres (6 miles) northwest from Manacor is the old farming town of Petra. Most visitors are American, for the town is the birthplace of Father Junípero Serra, founder of a chain of important missions along the American Pacific coast that evolved into today's cities of San Diego, Los Angeles, San José and San Francisco. This energetic Franciscan friar can probably be regarded as the founder of California.

Petra is a sleepy little place, something of a warren of tiny streets filled with attractive stone houses and ancient buildings. However its main attractions are well signposted, so there is little chance of getting lost.

Museu and Casa Junípero Serra ★★★

The museum contains superb wooden models of Fra Junípero's nine missions founded between 1769 and 1782 in that part of Mexico that later became California, and tributes from today's Californians. You can also see where he was born, an achingly simple house plus a tiny garden. Opposite is the Carrer California, the entrance to the 17th-century **Convent de Sant Bernadó**, where you can see a superb set of painted tiles set off by traditional wrought iron that show the achievements of this indefatigable evangelist. Museum and house open daily; times vary – tel: 971 56 10 28 for further information.

FATHER JUNÍPERO SERRA

A humble missionary of the Order of St Francis, Serra was born in Petra in 1713. He emigrated to Mexico in 1749 and lived there until the age of 54, when he was sent on a dangerous mission by King Carlos III. Serra accompanied the Spanish military to establish territories in what was to become California. Despite very tough conditions, Serra founded nine missions from San Diego to San Francisco. A further 12 were built in his name after his death in 1784. Spain eventually lost its new territory to Mexico in 1822 but the missions remain and the Catholic faith continues to thrive. A statue of Father Serra now stands in the Hall of Fame in Washington DC.

Opposite above:
Artificial pearls are big business in Manacor.
Opposite below: *The clocktower of Manacor's Església del Dolors.*
Left: *A charming hand-painted tile paying tribute to the 18th-century missionary Father Junípero Serra.*

Above: *The church of Sant Miquel, Felanitx.*

THE CHARCOAL INDUSTRY

Mallorca's hillsides are dotted with holm oaks, which used to provide a meagre living for families making charcoal. These families spent whole summers on the mountainsides, burning logs day and night to produce charcoal for sale. Anyone walking through the woods may stumble across a circular mound ringed, with mossy stones, which is a *sitja*, an old charcoal burning fire. Occasionally, the ruins of a charcoal burner's stone hut will be found nearby.

Felanitx ★

In the opposite direction from Manacor, 13km (8 miles) to the southwest, is the thriving town of Felanitx. Good, robust and rustic pottery is made here and you should be able to pick up some bargains at the Sunday morning market.

The town is dominated by the honey-coloured church of **Sant Miquel**, parts of which date back to the 13th century. The elegant Baroque west front, standing at the top of an imposing flight of steps, dates from the 17th century. Felanitx used to be famed for its cartographers and Mallorcans claim they provided the maps used by Christopher Columbus on his 1492 epic voyage of discovery. Try the local *ilet* in one of the bars – a drink made from milk, sugar and cinnamon, generally used as a hangover cure.

Villafranca de Bonany ★

Due west of Manacor on the main road back to Palma lies a charming village called Villafranca de Bonany. Anyone who takes cooking the least bit seriously should make a special pilgrimage here to buy fresh peppers, garlic or aubergines. More practically, sun-dried tomatoes are a little easier to take home on the plane.

Nearby lies the **Ermita de Nostra Senyora de Bonany**. It's easy to spot, for a huge statue of Christ surmounts the dome. Inside you will find a grotto with a Nativity scene. Outside there are superb views over the surrounding countryside.

Central Plain at a Glance

The Central Plain is at its best in **spring** or early **autumn**, when temperatures are pleasant and the fields are full of blossom or crops. During the summer it can be relentlessly hot and arid while winter nights may be rather chilly.

GETTING THERE

All locations are within easy distance of Palma, reached by good main **roads**. The main towns are fairly close to each other and all are well served by **buses**. A **train** service runs from Palma to Inca, stopping at Santa Maria and Binissalem on the way. The secondary country roads can be a little dusty and bumpy at times.

GETTING AROUND

You can hire a **car** or get around by **bus**. There are organized **tours** from the resorts to the main towns such as Inca and the pearl factories at Manacor; ask at your hotel or local tourist office for information.

WHERE TO STAY

There are few hotels in the Central Plain: visitors tend to come on day trips or stay in *fincas* – converted farmhouses. If you wish to stay in a *finca*, contact the Associació Agroturisme Balear (*see* below).

LUXURY
Es Reco de Randa, Font 13, Randa, tel: 971 66 09 97,

fax: 971 66 25 58. Lovely, traditional Mallorcan manor house. Swimming pool and an excellent restaurant.
Hotel Barcelo Ponent Playa, Cala Ferrera, Felanitx, tel: 971 65 77 34, fax: 971 65 80 86. Large 3-star family hotel with swimming pool and mini-golf.

MID-RANGE
Tamarix, Avda. Cala d'Or, Felanitx, tel: 971 65 78 51, fax: 971 65 90 09. Two-star hotel; swimming pool and bicycle hire.

BUDGET
Monasteri Cura de Randa, Puig de Randa, tel: 971 12 02 60. Cheap, basic acommodation in this tranquil monastery. Fully booked during the summer.
Jacinto, Weyler 1, Manacor, tel: 971 55 01 24. Small, basic hotel opposite the cathedral.

WHERE TO EAT

Inca has a particularly good selection of restaurants that make imaginative use of the abundant fresh vegetables grown in the region.
Cal Dimoni, Ctra. Manacor, Algaida, tel: 971 66 50 35. Huge, unpretentious, popular Mallorcan restaurant.
Celler Can Amer, c/Miquel Durán 35, Inca, tel: 971 50 12 61. Attractive *celler* that serves excellent Mallorcan food.
Inn de Son Fuster, Plaça d'Espanya, Inca. Roast suckling

pig is the house speciality.
Raco, c/de Dureta 1, Inca, tel: 971 50 30 15. Small, family run bar/restaurant.
Moli d'en Pau, Carretera Santa Margalida, Petra, tel: 971 85 51 18. A memorable Mallorcan experience: local food eaten in a converted windmill.
Es Cuatre Vents, Ctra. Manacor, Algaida, tel: 971 66 51 73. Fantastic range of Mallorcan food, very popular – essential to book for Sunday lunch.
Sa Gaflet, Ctra. Manacor, Algaida, no telephone. Try the stuffed mussels.
Son Colom, on the road to Campos, 1km (½ mile) west of Felanitx, tel: 971 58 10 76. A convenient place to stop if you are touring the area.

TOURS AND EXCURSIONS

Full-day and half-day tours leave Palma for Inca and Manacor. If you're staying in one of the resorts, check with your travel agent or local tourist office to see whether they organize trips as well.

USEFUL CONTACTS

Tourist Information: Gual 31A, Manacor tel: 971 82 09 31.
Associació Agroturisme Balear, c/Foners 8, Palma, tel: 971 77 03 36, fax: 971 46 69 10.
Real Aeroclub de Baleares (parachute jumps and trips in small aircraft) Aeródromo de Marratxi, tel: 971 60 01 14.

9
Menorca

The easternmost island in the Balearic archipelago, 34km (21 miles) from Mallorca, Menorca is smaller and quieter than its neighbour and has a more subtle appeal. The interior is green and undulating; scented pinewoods merge into grazing for the island's 25,000 dairy cattle and cycling tracks criss-cross the meadows and scrubland. The north coast is jagged and rocky, while the south coast, home to most of the resorts, is a string of soft, sandy coves sheltered by rugged headlands and cliffs.

Menorca's various colonists have left their legacy all over the island, which is littered with *talayots* and crumbling foundations of Bronze Age settlements. More recently, the three waves of British occupation have left Georgian architectural features, herds of black and white Freesian dairy cows and a thriving gin manufacturing industry. There are even a few rather incongruous English words in the Menorquí dialect.

The two main centres of population are **Maó**, the walled capital, nestling at the end of a massive natural harbour on the island's east side and **Ciutadella**, the ancient capital at the opposite end of the island. Maó is a busy port with lots of British architectural features, while Ciutadella is a graceful, aristocratic town with a maze of old, narrow streets and several beautiful churches.

Menorca's big resorts, like **Cala en Porter** and **Arenal d'en Castell**, offer all the usual trappings of bars, shops and restaurants, although escape is easy – to places like the pretty fishing village of **Fornells** and the breathtaking **Cap de Cavallería**, a steep headland in the far north.

SPAIN
MENORCA
EIVISSA
MALLORCA
FORMENTERA
ALGERIA

CLIMATE

Menorca is the wettest of the Balearic islands; there is plenty of winter rain but it doesn't get very cold. Spring, early summer and autumn also have overcast rainy days. July and August are hot and sunny, with temperatures comparable to Mallorca's.

Opposite: *Holiday-makers relax in the azure waters of Cala Santa Galdana.*

TOP ATTRACTIONS

*** **Ciutadella:** Menorca's beautiful, atmospheric old island capital.
*** **Maó:** modern capital with rich naval history.
*** **Naveta d'es Tudons:** the oldest surviving roofed building in Europe.
** **Binibequer Vell:** exquisite recreation of a Moorish fishing village.
** **North Coast Beaches:** deserted, sandy coves, unspoilt by tourism and accessible only by boat or on foot.

Maó

The area now occupied by Maó is documented as being settled as early as 800BC by Phoenician traders, who used Menorca as a staging post en route to the northern Mediterranean. Now the island's capital, Maó has a population of approximately 25,000 and is a lively, pleasant town with distinctive, British-influenced Georgian-style architecture, where whole streets – notably Carrer and Hannover – wouldn't look out of place in London. Maó has the largest natural harbour in the world after Pearl Harbour.

The town stretches out along the south side of the vast inlet, the north side dotted with luxury villas. Maó's harbour mouth is guarded by an imposing promontory, **La Mola**, now a military zone, and the remains of **Sant Felip fort**, a military museum. Both serve as a reminder of Menorca's former significance as a port of call; look at the peaceful scene today and try to imagine the year 1801, when 1165 large ships were recorded to have entered the harbour.

City Sightseeing

Maó is unquestionably a city to explore on foot, its impenetrable one-way system and tiny, narrow roads making driving impractical. Distances between the main sights are short and there are sufficient cafés dotted around the leafy squares for rest stops.

Plaça de S'Esplanada *

Begin at the tree-shaded Plaça de S'Esplanada at the top of the town, a pleasant square where the tourist office is located and locals meet at the various cafes and restaurants. The square is dominated by an old military barracks and some splendid 18th-century mansions, once lived in by wealthy British traders and officials.

Above: *The historic port of Maó, strategically important for hundreds of years.*

Most of the main shops are located on Carrer des Ses Moreres (also known as Carrer de Dr Orfila), which extends from the Plaça de S'Esplanada to the top of the steps leading down to the harbour. The street is a pedestrian zone.

Ateneu *

The Carrer del Comte de Cifuentes begins at the northwest corner of Plaça de S'Esplanada and here, at number 25, is the Ateneu, Maó's science museum. Visitors can see an eclectic collection of seashells, seaweed, rocks, stuffed birds, ancient maps, paintings and various objects relating to Menorca's own artistic life. It is run by the local cultural and historical society who are welcoming and enthusiastic. Open 10:00–14:00, 15:00–19:00 daily.

Santa María **

The city's main landmark, the church of Santa María, is located in the Plaça de la Constitució, straight down the hill from Plaça de S'Esplanada towards the harbour. The church dates from the 13th century but was rebuilt by the British in the 18th century, then sacked during the Spanish Civil War. Centrepiece within the church is the 3200 pipe organ, built in Austria in 1810, and the focus for Maó's Organ Festival in July.

MAYONNAISE

Menorca's culinary gift to the world is mayonnaise, named after Maó where it was first invented. Whether this was under French rule, or the French merely recognised a good thing when they tasted it, remains unclear. All that can be said is there can be no possible excuse for a restaurant on Menorca serving you anything other than fresh mayonnaise – made with olive oil, egg yolks and a touch of lemon juice, possibly a little freshly ground black pepper and sea-salt, garlic or fresh herbs to add extra flavour.

Ajuntament **

Just around the corner from the church of Santa María is the Ajuntament, or Town Hall. This neo-Classical building dates back to 1633 and was restored in 1788. Today, it proudly displays a present from the 18th-century governor Sir Richard Kane, a huge clock made in London. Inside there are portraits of Menorcan dignitaries and past French and Spanish governors. Look for the Carrer Port de Sant Roc and follow it until you come to the Port de Sant Roc, a gate that was part of the 16th-century walls built to repel Barbarossa, the infamous Mediterranean pirate.

Església del Carmen **

A few blocks away is the Plaça del Carmen, where the Baroque Església del Carmen church is worth a visit for the colourful market held in its cloisters, stalls of fruit and vegetables situated between graceful pillars. Look out for cheese and the local *sobrasada* sausage here. The fish market is nearby and is a hive of activity in the mornings, although you have to get there early before the day's catch is sold out.

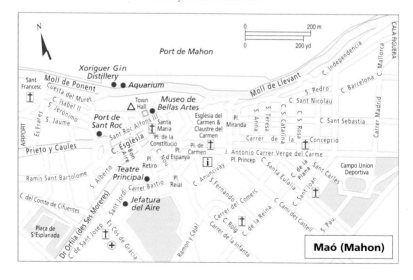

Maó (Mahon)

Church of San Francesc *

Go back to the Plaça de la Constitució and head 200m (220 yds) northwest down Carrer Isabel II. At the end is Sant Francesc, an 18th-century church with an unusual Romanesque-Baroque facade. Inside, the chapel of the Immaculate Conception is in an astonishing, fanciful style known as 'churrigueresque', full of florid details that provide a total contrast to the traditional, rather sober Spanish Baroque churches.

Waterfront **

A stroll along Maó's waterfront is full of colour and interest. Note the *llauds*, the unique Balearic fishing boats whose bow and stern are equally pointed, and which are still made to an ancient Arab design. Many of the houses along the waterfront have been actually built into the cliffs, which themselves are riddled with caves. Around the point of Moll de Llevant is the yacht mooring of **Cala Figuera**, a lively place for a sunset drink, browsing the shops and checking out the fish restaurants for dinner.

Xoriguer Distillery **

A legacy of British occupation, the 18th-century Xoriguer Gin Distillery is located on the Moll de Ponent harbourfront. Visitors can admire the huge copper stills bubbling to produce the spirit which is eventually blended with juniper berries to make the fragrant Menorcan gin. Visitors are encouraged to sample the gin and gin-based liqueurs, which include *palo* (made from carob seeds); *hierbas* (flavoured with camomile) and *calent* (tasting of aniseed, cinnamon and saffron). Open 08:00–19:00 Monday–Friday; 09:00–13:00 Saturday. There's a small aquarium, located near the gin distillery, that doubles up as a bar from 21:00 onwards – visitors can enjoy a drink amongst the fish tanks.

BRITISH BUILDINGS

The British influence is most marked in the east of the island, in and around Maó, where many of the old, Regency-style houses could have been transported directly from London or Bath. The Menorcan dialect contains many English architectural words: sash windows in those same Georgian mansions are known as *winders*; bow windows are called *boinders*; while the elaborate side-boards still found throughout the island are called *saydbors*.

Below: *Menorca's thriving gin-producing trade is a direct legacy of British rule.*

Above: *The wide mouth of Maó harbour is dotted with small islands.*
Opposite: *Motorboats in the creek at Port d'Addaia.*

Harbour Tours ★★★

Several important sights are located around Maó's vast harbour and the best way to see and photograph them are from the water. The tour takes an hour and tickets can be bought from the Xoriguer gin distillery showroom.

There are several British-built buildings overlooking the harbour, among them the distinctive **Hostal Almirante**, a Georgian villa once inhabited by Nelson's second-in-command Admiral Collingwood, and now a hotel. There's also the old customs house and **Golden Farm** where, according to legend, Nelson himself once stayed.

Villa Carlos ★

Almost a suburb of Maó, Villa Carlos, also known as Es Castell, lies east of the city by the water. This was the home of the British army garrison, whose principal function was to man the massive Sant Felip fort at the harbour mouth. Destroyed by the Spanish in 1802, the fort's grass-covered remains can still be seen. The town of Villa Carlos retains its original grid system and various British features, including the **Georgian Town Hall**, built by the then Governor, Sir John Mostyn, in 1771. The nearby district of **Cala Fonts** has some excellent restaurants.

Several islands are scattered around the vast harbour. **Illa del Rei** once housed a Roman villa and much later, in 1287, was the first part of Menorca to be freed from the Moors when King Alfonso III landed there. The **Illa Plana** was once a quarantine island, then a US naval base and later a base for the Spanish army. A third island, **Lazareto**, later took over the role as quarantine island and has dense walls, built to prevent infectious diseases from blowing over the town.

NORTH OF MAO
S'Albufera ★★

About halfway between Arenal d'en Castell and Maó is the freshwater lake and bird sanctuary of S'Albufera, a protected wetland rescued by environmentalists from the clutches of developers. The embryonic Shangri-La timeshare resort is the subject of many political tussles, as several of the houses have been built, but meanwhile the lake continues to thrive as home to thousands of ducks and heron. Over the sand dunes is the fishing village of **Es Grau**, which has an excellent beach. From here, you can also visit the islet of **Illa d'en Colom**, named not after Columbus, for once, but a particularly bloodthirsty pirate.

Port d'Addaia ★

A couple of kilometres east of Arenal is the yacht haven of Port d'Addaia, set at the end of a deep inlet, its mouth guarded by a sprinkling of islands, nesting site for masses of gulls in spring. This inlet has an exciting history: Roman amphorae have been found on the sea bed, an indication of the commercial traffic that visited Menorca centuries ago and in 1861, three Dutch ships were wrecked here, all of them carrying a cargo of gold and silver ingots. Addaia was the site of the last British invasion of the island in 1798.

Arenal d'en Castell ★

The busiest resort on the island's eastern side, Arenal lies on an attractive sandy bay 17km (10½ miles) to the north of Maó, its beauty only slightly marred by a necklace of high-rise hotels. The coastline on this side of the island has an almost sunken, fjord-like appearance and winds around in a complex system of huge natural inlets and craggy headlands.

SIR RICHARD KANE

Sir Richard Kane was Menorca's most influential English governor. He established Maó as the capital and built the road that links it with Ciutadella. He also imported the Friesian cattle that now seem so much part of the Menorcan landscape, established a more organised system of agriculture and had a great deal to do with the development of Menorca's gin industry. Maó grew to be one of the world's great entrepot ports, handling ships from all over the globe.

Above: *The rugged coast of Menorca is peppered with rocky coves.*
Opposite: *Dazzling white houses in the Moorish-style village of Binibequer Vell.*

Fornells *

Around the headland to the north of Arenal, the unspoilt fishing village of Fornells boasts a fish restaurant called Es Plau, reputed to be one of King Juan Carlos' favourites. Not surprisingly, fish farming is a major industry, but tourists are more attracted by the beaches outside Fornells, and possibly by the number of rare birds to be seen. An old watchtower overlooks the massive inlet guarded by the village and a short walk up here rewards the visitor with sweeping views of the coastline as far as **Ses Salines**, a gently shelving sand beach at the most protected end of the bay, popular with novice windsurfers.

The northern coastline is wild and undeveloped, green pastures giving way to scrubby hillsides covered with purple heather. A couple of minor roads lead to the more densely inhabited bays but otherwise, visitors have to make do with farm tracks and footpaths to get down to some of the exquisite, deserted bays. The **Cap de Cavallería** is the island's northernmost tip, from where there are breathtaking sea views.

Cala Pregonda **

On the coast beyond **Cap de Cavallería** lie three of Menorca's finest beaches: **Cala Pregonda**, **Cala en Calderer** and **Cala del Pilar**. There is a small river running into the sandy coves of Pregonda, also a track that leads inland to Mont Santa Agueda on which stand the remains of a Roman citadel, last used by Moors holding out against Alfons III.

Cala Pregonda is one of the island's best kept secrets, largely because there is no road access to it and no beach facilities. A very worthwhile 20-minute scramble from the nearby village of **Binimella**, the beach is idyllic: golden sands, dramatic sandstone rock formations and dense pinewoods providing shade during the heat of the day. Most of the visitors stay on board their yachts and the atmosphere is blissfully peaceful.

CALA MORELL CAVES

Seven kilometres (4½ miles) north of Ciutadella are some of Europe's most important late Bronze Age caves in Europe. Carved by man out of rock, some are surprisingly sophisticated, with windows, sleeping quarters and chimneys. They were originally troglodyte dwellings but after 1000BC were used as necropolises where funeral urns were stored. One has an elaborate façade.

South of Maó
Trepucó **

Around 6km (4 miles) south of Maó the main road runs directly to Sant Lluís, past the prehistoric side of Trepucó which contains one of the island's largest *taulas*. In the northern part of the excavation are the remains of the fortifications built in 1756 by the French Duc de Richelieu as he was besieging Sant Felip fort, then occupied by the British. The French had little respect for Menorca's cultural heritage and the duke allegedly used the top of the *taula* as a lookout post for lining up his guns on the fort.

Sant Lluís *

Packed with lovely white houses, Sant Lluís was founded after Menorca had been conquered by the French in 1756, led by the same Duc de Richelieu and named after Louis XV, serving as the French army headquarters during the Seven Years' War (1756–63). The streets have French names and the royal coat-of-arms of France is carved in the Baroque parish church.

There is a splendid windmill, the **Mola de Dalt**, opposite the Plaça Nova, that is now used as an agricultural museum. Sant Lluís also has a racetrack and a football stadium.

> ### FRENCH CONNECTION
>
> The summer of 1756 was a bleak time in the annals of British naval history. Admiral Byng, in charge of the fleet, was supposed to relieve General Blakeney at Sant Felip fort, who was being besieged by the French. However Byng turned tail at the last minute and Blakeney was forced to surrender to the Duc de Richelieu. Menorca was lost to the British for seven years and Admiral Byng was later executed for cowardice.

Binibequer Vell ***

To the south of Maó, several holiday resorts line the coast, **Cala d'Alcaufar** and **S'Algar** being two of the most popular. The shoreline here is rocky with small, sandy beaches lined by holiday villa developments. During the summer, the breeze is refreshing but can whip up into a sand-blasting wind.

About 12km (7½ miles) from the capital, the experimental village of Binibequer Vell is worth visiting, a dazzling cluster of white, Moorish-style houses along incredibly narrow streets, scarlet geraniums cascading from every balcony. Rather than building a soulless timeshare, Binibequer's Catalan

Right: *The ancient cave of Cala en Porter is an unusual setting for one of Menorca's nightclubs.* **Opposite:** *Sleek yachts sail round the cove of Cala Santa Galdana.*

developers wanted to create a living community with bars, squares and quirky architectural features like shady archways and a tiny harbour. There's a steeple – but no church. The results are impressive and there are some good beaches nearby at **Biniparratx** and **Binidali**.

Cales Coves ★★

West of Binibequer along the coast is the resort of **Cala en Porter**, one of the island's longest established resorts with steps leading down to a sandy beach. Just to the east of the resort are the famous **Cales Coves**, a honeycomb of ancient *talayotic* burial caves in the cliff face, dating from 800BC. The cave called De Jurats bears faded, almost illegible Latin inscriptions and others, which were inhabited much later, around the fourth century BC, have ledges and makeshift patios. Today the caves, which overlook two shingly beaches, are inhabited by assorted hippy groups, not entirely to the satisfaction of local residents.

The next big resort complex, **Son Bou de Baix** and **Sant Jaume**, sprawls along the straight, sandy **Platja de Son Bou**, backed by rolling dunes and favoured by locals from the inland town of Alaior, 9km (5 miles) away.

This entire stretch of the southern coast is one delightful cove after another – but many are best reached by boat as there is no major coastal road. Many of the better known beaches offer hire-boats for this reason – **Cala en Bosc**, which can be reached by road from Ciutadella, provides this service and is also a popular sailing centre.

Cala Santa Galdana *

The beautiful cove of Cala Santa Galdana is shaped like a half moon and serves a thriving resort, one of the most popular on Menorca. Leading north from the resort is the impressive **Barranco d'Algendar**, arguably the island's most dramatic limestone gorge, steep sided and densely vegetated. Birdlife in the gorge is fantastic and red kites, Egyptian vultures and booted eagles can all be spotted, while brilliantly coloured butterflies flit between the wildflowers.

Cala en Turqueta **

Cala en Turqueta is one of the island's prettiest beaches, unspoilt by development and accessible only via a rough road leading from the farm of Sant Francesc, 4km (2½ miles) from Sant Joan. White sand, aquamarine water, intriguing sea caves and shady pines make this a perfect spot and the only visitors are usually a handful of yacht passengers and anyone who has bothered with the walk. Also worth making time for is the stroll through the pine woods to the **Atalaya d'Artruix**, an old lookout tower with views across to Mallorca.

> **MENORCA AND THE ENVIRONMENT**
>
> In 1993 Menorca was declared a Biosphere Reserve by UNESCO in recognition of its environmentally sensitive development. Some 40% of the island is now protected by the Law of Natural Spaces and no development is permitted in fragile ecosystems like the lake of S'Albufera d'es Grau. The result is an island with some of the cleanest beaches and clearest water in the Mediterranean as well as a thriving community of wild migratory birds.

Above: *Convent at the top of Mont Toro, Menorca's highest peak.*
Opposite: *The megalithic burial tomb of Naveta d'es Tudons, shaped like an upturned boat.*

CENTRAL MENORCA

Prehistoric remains are scattered across the centre of Menorca, dotted in the fields either side of the main road which runs between Maó and Ciutadella.

Alaior *

12km (7½ miles) out of Maó, Alaior has two main industries: cheese-making and, courtesy of the British, shoe-making. The town dates back to 1304 and has a fortified parish church, reinforced by the villagers after Turkish pirates sacked Ciutadella in 1558. Alaior has an unusual claim to fame: a wave of emigrations from here in 1768 to the then British colonies in America culminated in the founding of the city of St Augustine in Florida, where Menorcan surnames can still be found.

Torre d'en Gaumes ***

Torre d'en Gaumes is the largest and most impressive prehistoric excavation on Menorca. Inhabited from around 1500BC right up until medieval times, the settlement would have been used to control the south coast of the island. Many of the solid structures are still standing including three *talayots* and the *taula* (table) area. Circular dwellings converge on a central courtyard, and down the hills a *hypostilic*, or pillared building, is in a remarkable state of preservation. No one knows the exact purpose of this construction but it is likely to have been used for storage.

Don't miss the ingenious water collecting system. Not only was water collected and stored via scores in the rock, but it was filtered by flowing though a series of pits where sediments would be deposited.

Es Mercadel *

Northeast of Alaior lies the town of Es Mercadel, overshadowed by Mont Toro. The main industries are shoes and biscuits, although you can also buy earthenware pots and straw hats.

ISLAND NAMES

The Greeks called the island Meloussa, or Island of Cattle, while the Phoenicians knew it as Nura, Island of Fire. When the Romans arrived in 123BC they called the island 'Minorca', or little one, as opposed to 'Majorca', the big one. Under the Moors the island was known as Minurka.

On the summit of Mont Toro is the **Santuari de Nostra Senyora de Toro**, a convent that celebrates a wild bull that led, many years ago, a party of monks to a hidden cave where they found a statue of the Madonna and Child. Sadly, an otherwise impressive array of radar dishes, radio and TV masts tend to intrude on ancient legends.

MENORCA

Ferreries *
Located 24km (14 miles) east of Ciutadella, Ferreries (from the Catalan for blacksmith) was once renowned for making iron door hinges; today it specializes in furniture and jewellery and makes an interesting shopping stop en route from Maó to Ciutadella.

Torre Llafuda *
Hidden among the trees close to the km37 marker, this partly excavated site reveals a couple of *taulas* (one broken), a *talayot* and a manmade cave in which there are Latin inscriptions. According to legend, a party of Moors who landed at Cala en Turqueta discovered gold coins hidden in a *tanca* here (a storage hole in the ground) and made off with it to their boat.

Torre Trencada *
A track off the main road at km39 leads to an impressive *taula*, a *talayot* and a series of burial chambers. The *taula* is unusual in that it has an extra support in addition to the table structure, and it is thought to have had magical significance in prehistoric times.

Naveta d'es Tudons ***
This Bronze Age burial chamber is one of the best examples of its kind and is situated on the main road near the km40 marker. Shaped like an upturned boat (from which it gets the name 'naveta'), the tomb was used for the storage of bones, arranged in two chambers alongside personal objects of the deceased, including bits of pottery.

RIDING

Equestrian events are extremely popular in Menorca, where there is no bullfighting. Trotting races take place in Maó and Ciutadella at weekends and are fiercely competitive, attracting international competitors. The jockey sits behind the horse in a small cart and must win the race without the horse breaking into a canter more than three times.
  Another typically Menorcan spectacle is a special kind of dressage involving prancing and controlled rearing, often demonstrated at island fiestas in the middle of a crowd. At the Doma Menorquina in Ferreries there are regular shows of these equestrian skills held for visitors.

CIUTADELLA

Ciutadella is one of the most exquisite little towns in the Balearics, a tangle of narrow streets radiating out from the Plaça d'es Born, a tree-shaded square and gathering place for locals. Virtually untouched by the tourism industry, the British or the French, the town retains Menorca's only traces of Moorish architecture, blending with the honey-coloured townhouses. The main road which bisects the old town has a lovely stretch of Moorish arches, **Ses Voltes,** under which tiny shops and restaurants have been accommodated.

Plaça d'es Born **

At the centre of Plaça d'es Born stands a poignant memorial to those who died when the Turks invaded in 1558, and to those whom the Turks captured and sold into slavery on their return to Constantinople, as it then was. The crenellated *ajuntament* (town hall) is on one side, opposite a row of magnificent 19th-century mansions built by the Torre-Saura family, just one of several palaces in Ciutadella. At the north end of the square, steps lead down to the picturesque harbour, with its host of small bars and cafes, many built into natural caves in the cliff side.

Old City ***

The Carrer Major, heading off Plaça d'es Born, leads into the old city, a place of colonnaded narrow streets whose style owes much to the town's Moorish past. Opposite the Palau Torre-Saura is the **Palau Salort** (open 10.00–14:00 Monday–Saturday), with an impressive, frescoed ballroom.

Further on the street leads into the Plaça de la Santa María Catedral, or Plaça Pius XII. Look for the side chapel with the Moorish arches, all that remains of the original mosque. The Olivar palace opposite the main entrance houses an art and archaeological collection.

Palau Squella *

Look, too, for Palau Squella, another aristocratic mansion, located on Carrer Sant Sebastian. Unfortunately the house is not open to the public, but its interest is that it contains a bed used by Napoleon I. The same bed was also used by US Admiral James Farragut, whose father emigrated to America. When the admiral visited the town of his ancestors in 1867, they made him an honorary citizen – and gave him Napoleon's bed to sleep in.

The Port **

Ciutadella's harbour is a tiny, narrow inlet, lined with bars and restaurants, many of which back into caves in the cliff face. Fishing boats and luxury yachts bob on the water and by night, the quayside is thronging with life. Fishermen unload their catch here twice a day, supplying the many restaurants.

MENORCA'S NIGHTLIFE

A 16th-century law demanded that all citizens of Ciutadella were asleep by midnight and in the 20th century, the town continues to shut down early. Menorca has always left the clubbing scene to Ibiza, although both Maó and Ciutadella are wonderfully atmospheric on a hot summer's night, buzzing with outdoor restaurants and pubs offering everything from jazz to karaoke. Venues for night owls include Cova d'en Xuroi, a disco in a cave at Cala en Porter; Sí and Caray in Maó; Pancha in Sant Lluís and Tonic on the Es Castell–Maó road.

Left: *The lovely old town of Ciutadella, once the island's capital.*

Menorca at a Glance

BEST TIME TO VISIT

Menorca has yet to suffer the overcrowding that can affect Mallorca so badly during the summer. Even so, August is the busiest month and it is essential to book accommodation in advance. During the winter months there is a cold, strong wind which blows from the north. Menorca is the wettest Balearic island; expect some cloudy days and rain in spring, early summer and winter.

GETTING THERE

Sant Lluís **airport** is less than an hour's flying time from Barcelona and two hours from London or Paris. There are several daily flights from Palma to Maó. The airport is 5km (3 miles) outside Maó and you'll have to take a **taxi** or hire a **car** as there are no connecting buses here. There is an excellent **ferry** service from Barcelona which takes about 9 hours. Inter-island ferries from Mallorca leave twice daily from Alcúdia to Ciutadella (4 hours) and once a week from Palma to Maó (6½ hours).

GETTING AROUND

A **bus** service plies the main road that stretches across the island linking the towns between Maó and Ciutadella; another runs from Maó to Fornells via S'Arenal. During the summer there are buses to the resorts. However, by far the best means of getting around the island is by **car**.

WHERE TO STAY

Accommodation is more expensive than on Mallorca. It is a good idea to arrange in advance, particularly if you're going in August; prices are inflated at this time as well. Maó and Ciutadella are the best places for bargains, but there's no guarantee of somewhere to stay if you turn up in peak season without a reservation. Most accommodation is in the resorts and the majority of people stay in holiday villas. *Fincas* are charming, converted farmhouses usually tucked away in the countryside; they are a more expensive option. Contact the Associació Agroturisme Balear (see below) for further information. Most places are shut between November and April.

Ciutadella
LUXURY
Patricia, Cami Sant Nicolau 90, tel: 971 38 55 11, fax: 971 48 11 20. Expensive but elegant.
Esmeralda, Cami Sant Niolau 171, tel: 971 38 02 50. Excellent 3-star hotel; most of the rooms have balconies with sea views; swimming pool, tennis courts.

MID-RANGE
Alfonso III, Cami de Maó 53, tel: 971 38 01 50. Moderately priced central hotel.
Hostal Ciutadella, Carrer Sant Eloy 10, tel: 971 38 34 62. This is a comfortable, modest hotel.

BUDGET
Paris, c/Santandria s/n, tel: 971 38 16 22. Basic but nice and comfortable, central position.

Maó
LUXURY
Port Maó, Avda. Fort de l'Eau, tel: 971 36 26 00, fax: 971 35 10 51. Spectacular 4-star hotel with excellent facilities; set in its own gardens overlooking the creek.
Almirante (Collingwood House), Carretera Villa-Carlos, tel. 971 36 27 00. The 18th-century official residence of Admiral Collingwood, now an excellent hotel; swimming pool, tennis court.

MID-RANGE
Hotel Capri, Sant Esteban 8, tel: 971 36 14 00, fax: 971 35 08 53. Open all year, modern 3-star hotel in the centre of Maó, attractive and well appointed.
Mirador d'Es Port, Vilanova 9, tel: 971 36 00 16, fax: 971 36 73 46. Reasonably priced 3-star hotel with swimming pool and good views.
Sol Mar de Menorca, Urb. Cala Canutells, tel: 971 15 31 00, fax: 971 15 30 32. Large, modern hotel with excellent facilities.

BUDGET
Hostal Orsi, c/Infanta 19 (off Plaça Reial), tel: 971 36 47 51. Central; bicycle hire available from here.

Menorca at a Glance

Hostal Roca, c/del Carme 37, tel: 971 35 08 39. Basic but it is central.

Hostal Sheila, Santa Cecilia 41, tel: 971 36 48 55. Family run, clean and good value.

Sant Lluis
MID-RANGE
Pension Xoroy, Playa Punta Prima, tel: 971 15 18 20. Idyllically situated amidst pine trees at the edge of the beach.

WHERE TO EAT

There are plenty of places where you can enjoy excellent Menorcan food. In Maó and Ciutadella there are good inexpensive café-restaurants – just stroll around the centre or along the harbourfront. The area around Fornells is well known for its seafood restaurants; the local speciality is *calderada de llagosta*, an expensive lobster stew.

Ciutadella
Casa Manolo, Marina 117, off the Plaça del Pins, tel: 971 38 00 03. Best restaurant in town; superb seafood and paella.

Ferreries
Vimpi, Plaça Principe Juan Carlos, tel: 971 37 31 99. According to legend the owner once worked in a Wimpy hamburger bar in London and borrowed the name when he went home. Someone objected, so he crossed off part of the first letter and came up

with 'Vimpi'. The name was all he brought back; the restaurant serves extremely good local dishes and excellent *tapas*.

Fornells
Es Pla, harbourfront, tel: 971 37 66 55. King Juan Carlos' favourite Balearic seafood restaurant and all you can say is that the man has excellent taste. The prices are a king's ransom too; even out of season you may need to book.

Maó
Jagaro, Moll Llevant, tel: 971 36 23 90. A good fish restaurant with expensive but adventurous dishes.

Rocamar, Cala Fonduco 32, tel: 971 36 56 01. There are lovely harbour views from this top-notch restaurant – booking essential.

Bar Europa, Carrer Cifuentes, tel: 971 36 13 79. One of the best *tapas* bars in the Balearics.

Mercadal
Can Olga, Pont Na Macarrana, off the Camino de Tramuntana, tel: 971 37 54 59. Traditional local food plus more than a few recipes of its own.

SHOPPING

Menorca is renowned for costume jewellery and leather goods; the best places to buy them are in Maó and Ciutadella.

Leather goods:
Marks, S'Arrivaleta 18 and Hannover 38, Maó.
Patricia, c/Ses Moreres 31/33, Maó.

Costume Jewellery
Bali, Carrer de Lluna, Maó.
Catisa, c/Sant Sebastian 75, Maó.

TOURS AND EXCURSIONS

Es Fornas, Box 842, Maó, tel: 971 36 44 22, organizes riding for both advanced riders and beginners.Don't miss the opportunity to see some of the *talayots* that are dotted around the island. If you have your own transport you can easily discover them for yourself.

USEFUL CONTACTS

Maó Airport: 971 36 01 50.
Radio taxis: 971 36 71 11.
Tourist Office: Plaça Explanada 40, Maó, tel: 971 36 37 90.
Associació Agroturisme Balear, c/Foners 8, Palma, tel: 971 77 03 36, fax: 971 46 69 10.

MAO	J	F	M	A	M	J	J	A	S	O	N	D
AVERAGE TEMP. °C	10	11	13	14	18	21	24	25	23	19	15	12
AVERAGE TEMP. °F	51	52	54	57	64	70	76	77	73	66	58	54
HOURS OF SUN DAILY	4	5	6	7	9	10	11	10	7	6	4	3
RAINFALL mm	60	49	48	47	30	19	4	30	63	105	92	85
RAINFALL IN	2.4	1.9	1.9	1.8	1.2	0.8	0.2	1.2	2.5	4	3.6	3.4
DAYS OF RAINFALL	10	9	8	8	6	4	1	3	6	12	10	10

Travel Tips

Tourist Information

The Spanish National Tourist Office has offices in the United Kingdom (57–58 St James' Court, London SW1A 1LD, tel: 0207 499 1169); the USA (665 Fifth Avenue, New York, NY 10022, tel: 212 759 8822, and offices in Chicago, Los Angeles and Miami); Canada (102 Bloor Street West, 14th floor, Toronto, Ontario, tel: 416 961 3131); Australia (203 Castlereagh Street, Suite 21a, PO Box A685, Sydney, NSW, tel: 02 264 7966) and in most European countries. For more specific local information there are *turismo* bureaux in both Palma and Maó.

Entry Requirements

EU citizens need a valid National Identity Card, with the exception of Denmark and the UK, citizens of which need a valid passport. UK visitors must have a full 10-year passport as of 1995. US, Canadian and Japanese citizens require a passport. Visas are required by citizens of Australia and New Zealand. For stays longer than 90 days a residence permit (*permiso de residencia*) is

required. EU citizens can apply for this in Spain; other nationalities need to get a special visa from the Spanish Consulate in their own country.

Customs

The maximum allowance for duty-free items brought into Mallorca and Menorca is as follows: one litre of spirits or two of fortified wine; two litres of wine and 200 cigarettes.

USEFUL PHRASES

Bon dia • Good morning
Bones tardes • Good afternoon/evening
Bona nit • Good night
Adéu • Goodbye
Com us deis? • What's your name?
Em dic... • My name is...
Té alguna habitació lliure • Do you have any rooms free
per una nit? • for the night?
Quant val? • How much is it?
Es car • It's expensive
A quina hora es pot sopar? • When do you serve dinner?
... berenar? • ... breakfast?
... dinar? • ... lunch?
Si us plau • Please
Gràcies • Thank you
De res • You're welcome

When bought and duty-paid in the EU, the amounts are 10 litres of spirits, 90 litres of wine and 110 litres of beer, for private consumption only. Both wine and beer are cheap locally so there is little point in bringing in either. There are no duty-free sales within the EU.

Spanish and foreign currency, banker's drafts and travellers' cheques can be imported and exported without being declared up to a limit of 1,000,000 pesetas. Spanish customs are usually polite and easy to negotiate but travellers coming in from Morocco are subject to stringent searches.

Health Requirements

No innoculations are necessary. The most common health hazards the visitor is likely to encounter are the occasional upset stomach and the effects of the sun, which is very strong during the summer months.

Free medical treatment is available to EU citizens on presentation of the appropriate form (E111 for British citizens). Visitors from outside the EU should arrange their own travel and medical insurance.

Getting There

There are regular flights to both islands from mainland Spain and from major European cities throughout the year. In the high season, charter flights arrive from North America. There are also daily inter-island flights which take under half an hour. Visitors arriving by plane in Mallorca arrive at the Son Sant Joan airport (tel: 971 78 90 99), 8km (5 miles) from Palma. The number 17 bus runs between the airport and Plaça d'Espanya in Palma. Menorca's airport is Sant Lluis (tel: 971 15 70 00), 5km (3 miles) outside Maó. It has few facilities and no bus service connecting it to Maó – you'll have to take a taxi.

A year-round ferry service from Barcelona and Valencia takes about 9 hours; during the summer there are daily connections to the islands. There are also ferries from Sète in France, Genoa in Italy and Algiers during the summer. The biggest ferry company is Transmediterránea, which has appointed agents in many countries (Palma tel: 971 70 23 00; Maó tel: 971 36 29 50; Barcelona tel: 934 12 25 24; Valencia tel: 963 67 65 12 for further information). There are also regular inter-island ferries.

What to Pack

Dress is casual on the islands, and in the summer many visitors spend most of their time in beachwear. Some restaurants and bars do not admit people wearing swimming costumes, so take something to cover up with. Four- and five-star hotels, and some night-clubs, may require a jacket and tie. Comfortable walking boots or shoes are useful for hiking in the mountains. In the cooler months of spring and autumn you should bring a sweater and a waterproof coat. Don't forget sunglasses and a sunhat. (*See also* Etiquette, p. 126)

PUBLIC HOLIDAYS

1 January •
New Year's Day
6 January •
Epiphany
March/April •
Good Friday, Easter Sunday, Easter Monday
1 May •
May Day
mid-June •
Corpus Christi
24 June •
Saint John (Saint James)
25 July •
Spain's patron saint
15 August •
Assumption of the Virgin
12 October •
National Day
November 1 •
All Saints' Day
December 6 •
Constitution Day
8 December •
Immaculate Conception
25 December •
Christmas Day

Money Matters

The Spanish currency is called the peseta. Coins come in denominations of 1, 5, 10, 25, 50, 100, 200 and 500; and notes in denominations of 200, 500, 1,000, 5,000 and 10,000. From January 2002, Euro coins and notes will be phased in. Banks and bureaux de change will always change travellers' cheques and foreign currency. Banking hours vary from city to city and town to town, but mostly it is from 09:00–14:00, although some will stay open until 16:30 in busy areas, and 09:00–13:00 on Saturdays. Banks are closed all day Sunday, national holidays and all Saturdays from July to October. You will need your passport for identification for any transaction you make at the bank. Most credit cards are accepted. Holders of cards bearing the Visa, Mastercard, Cirrus and Plus signs can use Spanish automatic tellers, which have instructions in English. IVA (Spanish sales tax) is 16% at the moment, and is not always included in the price so keep this in mind.

Always leave spare change (50–100 pesetas per person) in the average restaurant or bar, even if service is included. Upmarket restaurants expect 10% of the bill. Taxi drivers and petrol pump attendants also expect a small tip, anything from 50 pesetas up.

Accommodation

There is a good range of accommodation available in Mallorca and Menorca, and a comprehensive guide to local accommodation (*Hoteles, Campings, Apartamentos*) is available from tourist offices. Hotels are rated with a star system, with five stars being the highest. *Gran luxe* signifies a particularly luxurious hotel. Apartment hotels have cooking facilities in the rooms, and are graded from one to four keys.

Six percent IVA (tax) is added to the hotel room price – 15% is added in 5-star hotels. *Fondas, hostales and pensiones* are more basic and are graded from one to three stars. The local authority is responsible for accommodation classification, so gradings may differ from region to region. Most villages have rooms to hire – look out for signs saying *'se alquilar'*. If you want to get away from it all, *monasterios or conventos* sometimes offer simple accommodation to visitors.

The one sure way you can guarantee value for money is to book your hotel directly through a travel agent who knows the islands well; most visitors have accommodation included in a pre-paid package deal. Another advantage to pre-booking is that from June to September accommodation is in short supply, with what there is at very high prices. It is worth considering a villa or holiday apartment – check with the Tourist Board before signing up with a package/tour company. When booking directly from overseas, always insist on a written confirmation, either faxed or sent via the post. Bear in mind that the majority of hotels close for the winter season, roughly from November to April but sometimes longer.

Eating Out

There is a wide variety of places to eat in Mallorca and Menorca. Restaurants serving full meals are graded from one to five forks according to price, or there are *comedores*, which

are more simple dining rooms. Other restaurants are called *cellers*, like wine cellars but not underground. A *marisqueria* specialises in seafood and an *asado* in barbecued food. Alternatively *tapas* bars, *tascas, bodegas, cervecerias* and *tabernas* are all types of bar where you will find *tapas* (snacks) and *raciones* (light meals). *Menú del dia* is the menu of the day, which all restaurants have to offer by law and can sometimes be very good value.

Transport

Mallorca's bus service is reasonably good, and the island even has a small train system with two small tracks, one scenic route north to Sóller and the other running more frequently

to Inca in the east. The train station is in Plaça d'Espanya in Palma, where the main bus terminal is also situated. In Menorca the bus route is limited to the main road that runs between Maó and Ciutadella and a few of the main coastal resorts. Bus timetables are posted at bus stops *(paradas)*, or are available from tourist offices. All public transport services are drastically reduced on Sundays and public holidays.

By far the best means of getting about is by car, particularly on Menorca. There is a choice of car hire companies on both islands, with offices both at the airports and in the main towns. Drivers have to be at least 21, and to have had a licence for a year. Most foreign drivers licences are accepted in Spain, including EU, US and Canadian licences. If you bring your own car you must obtain a green card from your insurance company, as third party insurance is compulsory. To reach some of the more isolated beaches in Menorca you will need a four-wheel drive vehicle.

An alternative is to rent a motorcycle. To ride a machine under 75cc you have to be 14 or over, and 18 or over with a licence for a motorbike over 75cc. Crash helmets are compulsory.

There are taxi stands in the towns, or a radio taxi service is available (Mallorca Taxi Radio, tel: 971 75 54 40 or Taxis Palma, tel: 971 40 14 14; Menorca tel: 971 36 71 11). All taxis are licensed and must use their meters unless you have previously negotiated a special price – but that will only be for a long journey.

Mallorca is also bicycle friendly, especially on the Central Plain and the eastern and southern coasts. There are some more challenging routes for the experienced cyclist, especially in the Tramuntana mountain range. You can hire a mountain bike in Palma, at Bimont, tel: 971 73 18 66, or contact the Balearic Cycling Federation, tel: 971 20 83 62. Cyclists in Menorca are best advised to use a mountain bike: tarmac roads often turn into rough tracks long before you reach your destination.

Driving: in Spain is on the right. Speed limits are signposted, and are 120kph

---

ROAD SIGNS

Autopista • Motorway
Calzada estrecha •
Narrow road
Curva peligrosa •
Dangerous bend
Ceda el paso • Give way
Despacio • Slow
Alto • Stop
Prohibido adelantar •
No overtaking
Prohibido aparcar •
No parking
Catalan is beginning to replace Spanish in all aspects of Balearic life, including road signs. For example:
Castilian • Catalan
La Puebla • Sa Pobla
Santa Margarita •
Santa Margalida
San Juan • Sant Joan
Mahon • Maó
Ciudadella • Ciutadella
The word *ciutat*, meaning city, is often used to refer to Palma.

(75mph) on the motorways (*autopistas*), 100kph (62mph) on main roads, 90kph (56mph) on other roads and 60kph (37mph) in urban areas. Seatbelts are compulsory in the front seats and, if fitted, in the back. If you are caught speeding you will probably have to pay an on-the-spot fine.

Parking: To park in the main cities you will need a ticket, which can be bought at a meter on the street or in a tobacconist's.

Petrol: Petrol is *gasolina*, unleaded *sin plombo*. Petrol stations are usually open from 06:00–22:00; however they are closed on Sundays and public holidays. On Menorca petrol stations are few and far between. Only the larger stations tend to be self-service.

Business Hours

Generally shops and businesses are open from around 08:30–13:00 then 16:00–19:00. However, shops in Menorca often open later after the siesta, at 17:00. In the resorts, souvenir shops stay open as late as 22:00 in the summer. Visitors are advised to adopt the Spanish siesta routine: expecting to have meetings or to go sightseeing is not appropriate during the early afternoon. Lunch is usually served from 13:00–16:00 and dinner from 20:00 (sometimes earlier for the benefit of tourists) to 23:00. Most Spaniards eat at 22:00 or 23:00 in summer, although earlier in winter. Bars and clubs stay open late in the coastal resorts.

Time Difference

Spain is on GMT+1 hour in winter and on GMT+2 hours from the last Sunday in March to the last Sunday in October.

Communication

Telephone: Spain's telephone system is extremely good and simple to use. If relying on public phones, a phone card will avoid the need for vast amounts of loose change – they can be purchased at all post offices, most news kiosks and small shops, even bars. Telephones marked *urbano* are for local calls only; those marked *international* are for overseas calls. *Cabina telefónica* phones are only found in major tourist areas; an operator gets the number for you and you pay after the call is over. Coin phones use 100, 25 and 5 peseta coins. Hotels usually charge extra for overseas calls made from your room, even if you dial direct.

If using a public phone to dial overseas, dial 07 for the international link and as soon as you hear the high-pitched, continual tone, dial the code of the country you want followed by the area code and personal number. To reach the operator dial 002. Reverse charge calls can be made: simply dial 9398 and ask the operator for a *cobra revertido*. But this can only be done from phones that accept incoming calls, not from a public phone. If calling Mallorca or Menorca from within Spain the code is 971, from outside Spain it is 71.

Post: Post offices (*correos*) are open from 09:00–14:00 and

16:00–19:00 Monday to Friday, and in the morning only on Saturday. Stamps, *sellos,* can be bought from tobacconists and shops that sell postcards. Letterboxes are painted yellow except at the post office where they are set into the outside wall. Those marked *extranjero* are for abroad, *insular* for Spain.

Electricity

The power system is 220 to 225 volts AC. Two pin, round plugs are used. Americans will need a transformer, British visitors an adaptor.

Weights and Measures

Spain uses the metric system.

Health Precautions

In summer use a high factor sun protection cream and wear a hat. If you get a stomach upset, drink bottled water. Take mosquito repellent.

Tap water is safe to drink though it can be heavily chlorinated. Most visitors prefer mineral water: *sin gaz* means still, *con gaz* is carbonated.

Health Services

Chemists *(farmacias)* have a green cross hanging outside, and are open during shop hours. They also operate on a rota system, so at least one in every area should be open 24 hours (the rota is displayed in the window and addresses and opening times are printed in the local newspapers). Spanish pharmacists are highly trained and can dispense medicines that are usually available only on prescription in other countries. EU citizens should always take their Form E111 with them. In addition there is a medical insurance scheme called ASTES which is run by the Tourist Board.

Hospitals:

Son Dureta, Andrea Doria 55, Palma, Mallorca, tel: 971 28 91 00.
Municipal, Cos de Gracia 26, Maó, Menorca, tel: 971 36 12 21.

Personal Safty

The only likely problem tourists will encounter is petty crime, such as pickpocketing and bag snatching. Follow sensible precautions: don't leave anything unattended in the car, at the airport or on the beach, carry your bag securely, don't wear ostentatious jewellery, don't carry valuables in open pockets, and use the hotel safe whenever possible. It can also be a good idea to keep a record of your passport, travellers' cheques and credit card numbers. Remember that some areas are very poor, so bag snatching is more of a temptation. If you are robbed go to the police to report it, if only for insurance purposes. Sexual harassment should not be a problem, and it is generally safe for women to walk around the resorts at night.

Emergencies

In emergencies, dial **091** for the Policía Nacional. If you need a police station, ask for *la comisaria.* In some resorts there are special tourist police, Policía Turistica. The Fire Service number is **085** (**080** in Palma) and general emergencies **112**.

Etiquette

Topless sunbathing is acceptable on the beaches. In the resorts people spend most of their time in beachwear. When visiting inland areas and cities more modesty should be shown. Cover bare legs and shoulders when visiting monasteries and churches.

Language

Catalan is a descendant of Latin, mixed with Castilian and French. Any effort to speak a few words in Catalan will be much appreciated. (see p. 122).

CONVERSION CHART		
FROM	**TO**	**MULTIPLY BY**
Millimetres	Inches	0.0394
Metres	Yards	1.0936
Metres	Feet	3.281
Kilometres	Miles	0.6214
Kilometres square	Square miles	0.386
Hectares	Acres	2.471
Litres	Pints	1.760
Kilograms	Pounds	2.205
Tonnes	Tons	0.984
To convert Celsius to Fahrenheit: x 9 ÷ 5 + 32		

INDEX